Soc... ...sophy

Library of Social Work

General Editor:
Noel Timms
Professor of Social Work Studies
University of Newcastle upon Tyne

Social Work and Social Philosophy

A Guide for Practice

Chris L. Clark

*Lecturer in Social Work
University of Edinburgh*

with

Stewart Asquith

*Lecturer in Social Administration
University of Edinburgh*

Routledge & Kegan Paul
London, Boston, Melbourne and Henley

First published in 1985
by Routledge & Kegan Paul plc

14 Leicester Square, London WC2H 7PH, England

9 Park Street, Boston, Mass. 02108, USA

464 St Kilda Road, Melbourne,
Victoria 3004, Australia and

Broadway House, Newtown Road,
Henley-on-Thames, Oxon RG9 1EN, England

Set in 10/11 Times Linotron 202
by Inforum Ltd, Portsmouth
and printed in Great Britain

W26336 £5.95 485

Library of Congress Cataloging in Publication Data

Clark, Chris L.

Social work and social philosophy.
(Library of social work)
Bibliography: p.
Includes index.
1. Social workers, Professional ethics for.   2. Social
service—Philosophy.   I. Asquith, Stewart.   II. Title.
III. Series.
HV10.5.C58   1985   361.3   84–11471

British Library CIP data also available

ISBN   0—7100—9630—5 (Pbk)
ISBN   0—7102—0610—0 (C)

Contents

Acknowledgements   vii

Introduction   1

1 The person and moral agency   6

2 Rights, self-determination, paternalism and authority   23

3 Moral and political theory in social work   46

4 Professional ethics and politics   82

5 Ideology in social work   101

Notes   121

Bibliography   123

Index   129

Acknowledgements

The idea for this book arose from a course which Stewart Asquith and I have jointly undertaken for social work students at Edinburgh University. Over the period of working together our thinking on the subjects addressed has become shared to the point where its ancestry can often not be clearly distinguished. The plan for a book began as a similarly joint project, but in the event personal considerations prevented Stewart Asquith from taking an equal part in carrying it out. The greater part of the execution therefore fell to me, and with it the responsibility for the book's shortcomings. My first debt however is to Stewart Asquith for introducing me to many key issues in social philosophy, for his clarity in dealing with false starts and errors, and for his moral and intellectual support. We both owe to our students constant stimulation and much constructive criticism in developing the topics which we shall take up here.

I would also like to record my warm thanks to Alastair Campbell for his valuable appraisal of a draft version. Noel Timms's percipient and meticulous editing has both added substance to the argument at various points, and in very many places helped me to express more clearly what I was trying to say.

Chris Clark

Introduction

The philosophy and practice of social work have recently attracted renewed scrutiny as a result of the latest of a long series of more or less official reviews. The legitimacy of the theoretical principles on which social work practice is based is being subjected to critical appraisal not only from individual authors concerned to promote a sounder foundation for social work, but also by government-sponsored bodies such as the Barclay Committee (1982). Social work is not alone in this respect and confidence in professional judgement and expertise in a number of fields, both in the welfare arena and more widely, as in health care, has been waning under the more general onslaught on 'welfarism'. The growth of delegated legislation in the welfare field since the 1960s, through which the quality of services is dependent upon the individual judgement of practitioners, has meant that there are many areas of life in which members of the public are subject to what is perhaps rather loosely referred to as 'professional judgement'. Social work is faced with the acute problem of whether in fact it enhances human freedom and welfare or restricts it. Concern has been expressed that intervention in people's lives albeit in the name of welfare may well be unwarranted, unjustified and indeed unjust. Where the legitimacy of the principles on which professionals such as social workers operate is challenged then questions about accountability, control and justification become crucial in the context of actual practice.

Social work possesses a moral and political dimension by the very fact of intervention in people's lives and, we shall argue, social work practice cannot be justified merely by reference to theoretical statements about human behaviour or interpersonal relationships. The justification must of necessity be in moral terms. And at a time when the legitimacy of social work is in question, the need for the individual social worker, and for social work as a body of knowledge, to offer justifications for decisions made is all the greater.

1

Introduction

The aim of this book is to provide social workers with a conceptual framework for understanding and analysing the moral and political questions that are inextricably linked to the practice of social work. The basis of the approach will be to draw from the concepts and methods of social philosophy and apply them to the analysis of social work practice. The major assumption underlying this book, and one that will be discussed in the course of it, is that social work is essentially a moral and political enterprise and elements of traditional moral philosophy are not alien to social work practice but are embraced by it. Biestek (1961, p. 100), though his view of social work may not hold generally in contemporary circles, identified the significance of the relationship between practice and more general moral concerns rather nicely:

> Caseworkers are not philosophers by profession and seem to have little inclination in that direction. However, since they enter other people's lives in a very practical and intimate way, they necessarily become involved in issues which have an inescapable connection with the philosophy of human living.

Just as social work must necessarily entail questions of personal morality, so also it cannot be anything other than a political enterprise. The problems encountered by clients are not to be understood purely by reference to their personal or private circumstances, but derive also from much broader social processes. Such broader concerns raise political questions to do with the supposed causes and cures of social problems. Any failure to maintain a theoretical link between the individual and society, the personal and the political, results in social work practice operating on the basis of unresolved ambiguities. The practice of social work raises moral and political dilemmas for the social worker in relation to his client; it also raises social and political questions concerning the role of social work as a professional activity in relation to society as a whole.

This book has grown out of a course on social work and social philosophy which we have given for social work students at Edinburgh University over a number of years. The course was inspired by a belief that the almost universally acknowledged importance of moral and political questions to social work practice was not matched by a sufficiently systematic or sustained dialogue about them in social work education or social work practice. Social work training, we believe, should include the opportunity to gain some competence, and confidence, in reflecting critically upon the moral and political issues involved. We are not suggesting that social workers should become philosophers; rather, that in forming an understanding of practice issues benefit would be gained from philosophical reasoning. Until very recently the treatment of this area in the social work literature has been all too fleeting and insubstantial; many texts devote a few non-committal pages to 'values' before hastening, with evident relief, to more down-to-earth matters. In other cases the treatment of 'values' is heavy with case histories but lacking in the analysis which brings usable generalisations within one's grasp. On the other hand much of the literature of social philosophy is cast in a tradition which many practically minded social workers find remote, dry and inaccessible.

Because we are convinced that many of the principal theories and traditions from social philosophy are crucially relevant to social work practice, in this book we apply those themes to the context of social work. Discussion of moral issues in social work has frequently been vitiated by an inadequate formulation of key concepts such as the person or self-determination, and here the discipline of a philosophical approach can help one to get beyond the slogan or the cliche to a more careful examination of what such notions might imply in actual practice. This book is aimed therefore at social work students and practitioners who desire a more substantial dialogue on the moral, ethical and political aspects of practice. We hope to provide a pathway for social workers into moral and political philosophy. With this audience in mind, we have generally used the social work vocabulary, despite the fact that it is often not altogether precise or satisfactory in ethical matters as in others. This short book may be thought of as a social work traveller's guide to social philosophy. Like all guidebooks, it is not a substitute for making the journey oneself, but it should help to make the trip more profitable. Equally, as with all guidebooks, the inhabitants of the areas described will probably find some parts of the presentation oversimplified or inaccurate. No previous acquaintance with philosophy is assumed, and philosophical technicalities have been avoided where doing so does not lead to excessive clumsiness or imprecision. Professional philosophers will find the content largely familiar but we hope its application to social work will help to sustain the essential dialogue between philosophy and practice.

It is not our primary intention to offer or propound any specific moral or political theory for adoption as a basis for practice, but rather to provide some analytical help to a reader who is trying to appraise the actions of others and work out his own commitment. Nevertheless we have obviously made significant choices of topic and approach, thus defining areas of relevance. In debating the substantive issues our own opinions will on occasion be more or less apparent. We do not present them here primarily to defend them, but in order to stimulate debate. It follows from what we have already said that any involvement with social work precludes total neutrality.

The topics which we shall take up in this book are complex in that theories and issues from one context often have important repercussions in another, and it is virtually impossible to disentangle them completely. For example, the idea of freedom involves questions both about what people ought or ought not to be allowed to do in a political sense, and rather different sorts of questions about whether it is sensible to talk about a human capacity to exercise freedom of choice in the face of evidence that our lives are determined by heredity and environment. But an analysis of such problems must break into the circle somewhere. In very broad terms, this book is structured on two main lines of development which are pursued simultaneously, and together provide a frame of reference within which the various topics are located. The first organising principle is to start with a focus on moral questions which are faced in the individual person's life, and move as it were outwards to a consideration of what principles should be used to regulate social and political life in the wider community. We believe this way of thinking will be familiar to social workers as the model that often underlies the teaching of assessment. The second organising principle is to begin with general philosophical questions about the nature and basis of morality and move by stages towards types of theories that lend themselves to practical application in life generally, and social work specifically. The reason for adopting these two organising principles is that it permits an explication of concepts and values which are already within the language of social work and with which most social workers have some degree of familiarity: for example, the person, rights and duties, social justice, professional ethics, ideology. Thus we analyse the interconnections and implications of major concepts which have a wide currency in social work but are too often treated as if they had some kind of independent, self-evident validity.

We now present an overview of the argument. In Chapter 1 we examine the notion of the person and the attributes of personhood. A view of personhood is presented which at least partly accounts for the concept of respect for persons, traditionally advocated as the fundamental moral principle of social work and other caring professions. However respect for persons as a principle does not by itself suffice to describe how one ought to treat persons, and therefore in Chapter 2 we analyse the rights of persons generally and those involved in social work in particular. A consideration of rights leads readily to a corresponding consideration of duties. On the basis of this analysis we then discuss a number of supposed rights and duties in social work, especially self-determination, paternalistic intervention, and the problem of authority.

The discussion of rights will demonstrate the conclusion that no full specification of rights, or resolution of the problems of conflicting rights, is possible without recourse to a general ethical and political theory. In Chapter 3 we summarise two major ethical theories, utilitarianism and deontology. This is complemented by a review of political values, notably justice and freedom, and of political theories, specially liberalism and socialism. Chapter 3 thus marks a transition in the argument from the 'personal' to the 'political', while reaffirming the essential theoretical and practical interdependence of the two. The chapter goes on to enquire into the influence upon social work of the different traditions discussed, and concludes with a suggestion on how some resolution of the conflicting theories might be attempted.

Chapter 4 returns to the theme of the relationship between knowledge, values and practice already alluded to above to conduct an enquiry into the significance of codes of ethics in social work. It will be argued that social work practice necessarily generates moral and political problems, and that these are not adequately comprehended by conventional lists of ethical rules. Theory and practice must embrace technical knowledge and practical action as well as moral principle. A version of the idea of praxis is presented which attempts to overcome the untenable demarcation between theory and practice.

The final chapter proceeds to an analysis of ideology in social work. Ideology is a valuable concept because among other things it integrates questions of knowledge and value which have figured in earlier chapters. The meaning of ideology is analysed, and ideology is posed as a direct counterpart to the idea of praxis developed in the previous chapter. Thence we comment further on the significance of ideology for social workers by means of a discussion of a number of contemporary ideological tensions in social work. These tensions are seen to re-echo or recapitulate concerns that have appeared throughout the book.

Chapter one

The person and moral agency

1 Knowledge and values in social work

> Even with hindsight it is permissible to ask whether all this
> psychological and sociological knowledge is not more of a
> hindrance than a help. (Ruth Wilkes on the Maria Colwell case,
> 1981, p. 92.)

> There is a real need for social work training to contain as part of
> the core curriculum a philosophical discipline capable of honest
> discussion of the presuppositions that underlie the various
> doctrines now in vogue. (Wilkes, 1981, p. 109)

Few social workers will be unaware of the repercussions of the
Maria Colwell case on debates about what social workers were
doing, or claimed to be doing. As a result of that case social workers
were invited to consider the justifications that might be offered in
adopting a particular course of action with their clients. Issues of
accountability, professional judgement, professionalism and inter-
agency cooperation were all brought more sharply into relief.
Questions of justification do not simply entail an assessment of why
a social worker acted or failed to act in a particular way, though they
may do when the social worker's professional competence is being
judged. What may often be involved or implied is a critique of the
very foundations of social work knowledge. Wilkes's point is that
more has to be involved in providing social workers with adequate
skills and techniques than acquainting them with knowledge
gleaned from the social sciences; indeed by itself such knowledge
may actually be harmful. The danger feared by Wilkes and others
(Campbell, 1981; Ragg, 1977) is that reliance on social scientific
knowledge is liable to be restrictive in that it may lead to losing sight
of the client as a whole person, and reductionist in that the attempt
to analyse human behaviour and social problems in too narrowly

'scientific' terms may result in a fallacious oversimplification of the richness and complexity of human experience and social life. That is, there may well be a direct conflict between what is widely taken to be the prime value underpinning social work, respect for the person, and the types of knowledge to which social workers are introduced in the process of training. It is a main premise of this book that social workers themselves need to be aware of the values and philosophical assumptions that guide their day-to-day practice. In agreement with Laycock it is our belief that

> Social work is in the peculiar position of having many worthwhile skills without either a coherent unifying philosophy or a sufficiently strong scientific foundation to subject skills to rational enquiry.

and that

> Increased emphasis on knowledge and research does not lessen the significance of the value-base. It is from this base that social work must search out the knowing which can help in realising its values in practice. (Laycock, 1981)

An adequate answer to the question 'why did you choose to do X?' cannot simply be in technical or instrumental terms such as 'because X is the appropriate form of action' or 'because recent research suggests that X will be more effective' or 'I learned to do X when I was on a social work course'. The answer must necessarily involve some form of value judgement such as 'because I believe X is morally right'. Social work practice can never be judged purely in terms of the technical appropriateness of particular strategies since practice is inextricably bound up with questions of value and morality. An interventive strategy might be demonstrably effective on the basis of social science knowledge but yet be unacceptable on moral grounds. For example it might conceivably be shown that prolonged solitary confinement increased compliance to authority in troublesome youngsters, but that would hardly serve to justify such a strategy. Furthermore, the social worker does not acquire some sort of general moral immunity by virtue of his position; he is still bound by most ordinary moral obligations towards the client as a fellow human being. Social work clients are individuals and social work entails personal relationships. For that reason, the client must be considered not merely as a unit upon whom the social worker can inflict his expertise but as a person who may on occasion need protection from the 'expert' and who in any case is to be treated according to the principles of everyday morality. Practice principles in social work are drawn from prescriptions from social science, the fruits of practice experience, and moral precepts, and some com-

7

mentators argue therefore that such principles have very similar objectives to a code of morals. As Lewis (1972) suggests:

> These practice principles define the performance expected of the principled practitioner and his commitment to a moral practice. Morality produced a set of values and seeks to generate trust and justice in reciprocal human relationships.

For social work in particular and morality in general the concept of the person and the maxim of respecting the person are central. In line with what has been discussed above it is our belief that the concept of respect for the person is no less valid in the contemporary context of social work than previously and that, indeed, because of the greater commitment to professionalisation and social science, the need for it may be all the greater. However, the notion of the person is a particularly malleable concept and it is to a fuller exploration of some of its meanings and the implications they may have for social work practice that we now turn.

2 Persons and moral agency

In terms of ordinary moral language, only those individuals who can be truly considered agents, that is who have the capacity to make decisions about their lives and act on them, can be deemed appropriate subjects of moral judgement or moral appraisal. The notion of the individual as a moral agent is particularly important for a number of reasons. In everyday language, moral discourse generally focuses on actions that have in some way deviated from accepted norms and standards. Questions about the moral responsibility of the individual arise when we feel that an individual has performed an action which he[1] ought not to have done or conversely failed to act in a way that we feel he ought to have. In order to be able to blame or censure this individual we have to be able to say that he acted freely of his own volition. Only freely acting and freely choosing individuals can be accepted as truly being moral agents. Inextricably related to the notion of the individual as a moral agent is the idea of freedom of action. This in itself is a problematic notion and the concept of freedom will be discussed in more detail below. But an important point has to be made here: that judgements of behaviour are essentially judgements about *human* action. For the purpose of moral judgement, how we identify an action for which a person can be held morally responsible depends on the conception of human nature employed. Those who have not the capacity for truly human action cannot be the subject of blame or moral censure and can be excused from moral judgement. Thus it may not be possible to say of a person suffering from one of a variety of mental illnesses that he acted freely when behaving in a way that is considered immoral or even illegal. It is on such a distinction that rests the differential treatment of those who break the law when in a state of insanity. Similarly, there are individuals whose status as moral agents is somewhat confused since they are not considered to have attained or retained the status of moral agents by virtue of, for example, their youth – as with children – or by virtue of senility or mental handicap. The general point being made is that the notion of being free to act is closely linked to the concept of moral agency.

A further implication of the notion of the individual as a moral agent is that the recognition of the individual as morally competent entails the belief that there are certain areas of his life where intervention is unwarranted. That is, the individual as a moral agent has the right to expect *freedom from* interference by others. Any intervention in his life even though it is designed to be in his best interests has to be based on the recognition that waiving the rights of the individual may be involved.

Of particular significance then in judging moral competency and moral agency is the extent to which the individual can be considered to be free to act. However there is considerable divergence among philosophers as to the best way of explaining human action. Broadly speaking two philosophical traditions have evolved. These are (i) libertarianism in which it is asserted that the agent acted of his own free will in that he could have done otherwise; and (ii) determinism which we take to mean that philosophy which asserts that for everything that happens, and this includes human action, there are antecedent conditions such that nothing else could have happened. The major difficulty for determinists is that since causal explanations do not appear to rest easily with moral language (if X had to happen then there can be no question of moral responsibility) it is difficult for them to sustain a notion of the individual as a freely choosing person. There is an apparent paradox between the determinist thesis of human action and the commonsense notion of agency and personhood. In this respect social work finds itself in a somewhat ambiguous position. Despite the principle of respecting the person, social workers, in the course of training and later in their professional capacity are invited to familiarise themselves with social science theories which are largely determinist in character.

It is particularly interesting that whereas the notion of respecting the person has been what Pearson (1975a) refers to as one of the 'constancies' of social work, theories of human growth and behaviour adopted by social workers have been in a continual state of flux and reflected the broader ideological attractiveness of such theories at particular points in time. However no one school of thought can be treated as providing definitive explanations of

9

human behaviour and it would therefore be dangerous to base social work tactics on a single set of theoretical principles. Furthermore, as Wilkes and Campbell have pointed out for the caring professions and as others such as Rogers and Laing have done more generally, deterministic explanations virtually deny the status of personhood by reducing behaviour to stimulus and response. It is perhaps not surprising that both Campbell and Wilkes in different contexts have argued that the concentration on scientific type theories is a poor basis for caring relationships and that the carer has at least to supplement that form of knowing with a degree of imagination, or even to reject it as a valid basis for practice.

A further problem associated with the concept of moral agency has to do with the mutual influence of individual and society. As individuals we never exist in isolation but are part of a larger collective including perhaps the family, the peer group, or society. The problem is how to take account of the effects of social structure and political constraints on the individual. For social work there is potential for conflict between the guiding principle of respect for persons – an apparently individualistic notion – and recognising the causal significance of social, structural, economic and political factors. The individual who is considered freely acting and choosing is doing so within the particular social and economic circumstances of his time.

3 On being a person and respecting persons

We have already seen that there is a divergence of views between those who adopt a libertarian conception of human agency and those who prefer determinist accounts. Yet such a dichotomy is not easy to sustain, for two reasons.

First, there is a further tradition in philosophy, often known as compatibilism, which suggests that libertarianism and determinism may not be irreconcilable. In fact, it is argued that the notion of free action without some notion of causal antecedents is totally meaningless. Individuals may be free to act according to choice but their choices are effectively determined by social and biographical factors. According to this view we must, even if determinism were true, employ concepts of rationality, moral responsibility and free will for the purposes of ordinary moral interaction.[2]

Second, though it is the capacity for moral action that distinguishes man from other phenomena, human beings are also subject to events in the world that are beyond their control. Even though Kant argued that man is a rational animal, he recognised that man is also a sensory animal in that he is endowed with a physical constitution. However, explanations of the rational element must not be confused with explanations of the corporeal.

In adhering to the principle of respecting the person just what is it that social workers are committing themselves to and how can it be reconciled with the contemporary tendency to explain human behaviour in essentially causal terms? The caring professions are involved in a practice which is inevitably performed within specific moral and political contexts and the merit of a principle such as respect for the person is that it structures our social relationships, either in society in general or in the caring context in particular, in a way that recognises that there is something unique about the individual as a person. Campbell (1981, p. 104) puts it well when he argues

> But the extension of the 'scientific' approach to individual caring relationships has grave dangers. As soon as we regard the person before us as one example of a whole set of similar 'cases' we blind ourselves to the uniqueness of his need for care. We restrict ourselves to offering a functional relationship in which our task becomes the matching of the correct treatment to the problem before us.

But social work both in theory and in practice may well employ assumptions which are in effect in total opposition to the principle of respecting the person. In deciding what form any proposed intervention in the life of another should take, the social worker must evidently base his judgement on some theory of human behaviour and some notion of human action. However, the principle of respect for the person, as we shall later discuss more fully, entails persons as ends in themselves and not merely as instances of various social and psychological phenomena. The major problem with determinist accounts of human behaviour is that they are generally unable to accommodate concepts which are generally maintained by non-determinists as characteristic of the status of personhood. Indeed, Skinner (1972) suggests that the concept of the person is an incoherent, anachronistic device employed to explain certain events in the world, human action, which can readily be accounted for in term of cause and effect.

We shall now explore various approaches to explaining or accounting for the person or the status of personhood by discussing some of what are taken to be characteristic attributes of a person. We shall see that the identification of an individual as a person necessarily entails the adoption of a particular stance. In some senses the notion of respecting the person is tautological since the concept of the person, it could be argued, necessarily entails respect.

The person and moral agency

(a) Persons as biological entities

One of the problems which troubles philosophers is the extent to which mental and subjective processes are dependent upon physical and bodily mechanisms. Two answers to the question have been given. The first is that bodily processes are distinct from subjective and mental elements and there is something unique about the individual as a thinking, conscious being; this is often referred to as the ghost in the machine view. Such a position, maintained by those referred to as Cartesian dualists, accommodates the concept of the person or the self as an entity in its own right. Persons on this viewpoint are what Chisholm (1976) refers to as 'entia per se'. The opposite position is that all events or states of affairs in the world including subjective elements and persons can be explained in terms of cause. Thus for example Skinner, a proponent of a particular brand of determinism, attempts to account for subjective states in terms of biological and physiological processes. It is worth noting at this juncture that the attraction of behaviourism is not only does it seek to explain how individuals come to behave as social and personal beings but it also provides a theoretical framework – learning theory – on which strategies to correct malfunctions of behaviour can be based. Social work has not been slow to respond to the appeal of a theory which embodies therapeutic prescriptions. A number of strategies in social work have been derived from learning theory and include for example the use of token economy systems in children's homes.

Nevertheless, to return to our purpose, the question we have raised is the extent to which in ordinary moral language we can define persons in terms of their physiological and biological endowments. There are a number of problems with such an approach and it is clear that it does not receive universal acceptance.

In 1973, the United States Supreme Court in the case of *Roe* v. *Wade* held, in discussing the question of abortion, that 'the unborn have never been recognised in the law as persons in the whole sense' (quoted in Feinberg, 1973b, p. 185). This would suggest that simply having the biological potential to attain personhood is regarded as insufficient to ascribe that status to the foetus. Alternatively, if we reject the court's view, the implication might be that abortion could be tantamount to murder. The status of the foetus and the reaction we adopt to it in terms of the legitimacy or otherwise of abortion are inextricably linked. Clearly, the foetus is not yet biologically independent and not yet fully a person but there is a strong movement to protect unborn children from abortion on the grounds that they have a right to life. More is required to identify a being as a person than simply biological make-up.[3]

Similarly, if we accept the determinist and in particular the biological and physiological position, there is prima facie little reason to respond to human beings whether born or unborn in a manner different from our reaction to other biological organisms. Yet in terms of our ordinary commonsense morality we do conceive of human beings as different from animals, though some such as Singer (1979) would argue that the logical consequence of this view is that we need to reappraise our moral stance to animals.

Further, as Campbell (1975) points out, there are attributes which we associate with persons, such as consciousness and rationality, which we neither associate with animals nor, and perhaps this is more important, which can be adequately explained by or accommodated within determinist theories. This does not mean however that the status of personhood is independent of physical characteristics.

(b) Persons as sentient beings

Human beings obviously have the capacity to suffer pain and experience a variety of emotions: that is, they are sentient beings. However, sentience as a necessary and sufficient characteristic of persons must surely be defective for the same reasons as we have discussed in the previous section. That is, there are many forms of human life which may well have all the features of being sentient but which in other respects cannot be called persons. Once again the unborn child in the context of abortion provides an example of an individual whose status as a person may be questioned though his status as a sentient being may not be challenged beyond certain limits. It is quite indicative that the attempts in the Corrie Bill for example to stipulate the period of pregnancy beyond which it would be wrong and illegal to perform an abortion hinge on the capacity of the foetus to experience pain. Both the biological and the sentience arguments are inadequate in that they fail to take account of the essentially human attributes. If, for example, in the case of abortion the killing of a sentient being is murder, then so also is the slaughter of animals.

(c) Persons as rational beings

In Kantian ethics, moral agents are of supreme value because they are capable of exercising reason, volition and choice. It is the belief in the capacity for reason which most clearly distinguishes Kantian philosophy from determinism. Here the definition of a person, the notion of moral agency and the idea of freedom are all inextricably bound up with each other. The practical exercise of reason is what

The person and moral agency

distinguishes man from other animals and for Downie and Telfer (1969, p. 20) practical reason is

> The ability to choose for oneself and, more extensively, to formulate plans and policies of one's own. A second closely related element is the ability to carry out decisions, plans or policies without undue reliance on the help of others.

Now clearly, we conceive of rationality as a characteristic of our fellow human beings. Indeed, the very ideas of morality and moral responsibility, as we have seen, demand that we believe that others as well as ourselves can make rational choices and evaluations of the consequences of their actions. However, although rationality may be one feature of persons this presents a problem for social workers who claim to abide by a principle such as that of respect for the person. The problem is that there are some individuals who are offered social work help, and to whom the principle is presumed to apply, of whom it may not incontrovertibly be said that they are able to act rationally in the sense of being able to make choices and act upon them without undue reliance on others. Amongst these could be included children, the mentally ill, the mentally handicapped, unborn children and so on. Indeed, to return to an earlier theme of this chapter, depending on the social and political theory employed by the social worker to account for social problems, it could even be argued that most clients are unable to exercise reason and act accordingly because their choices and the means for expressing them are effectively limited by the social, political and economic conditions under which they live. For the Marxist, clients may be conceived of as the victims of social structural forces which deprive them of the opportunity truly to exercise their reason in accord with their will; though he may still wish to adhere to the principle of respect for persons.

(d) Persons as self-conscious beings

Whatever we may say about the physical attributes of persons, we also credit them with the mental faculty of consciousness. That is, they have the capacity for self-awareness, self-reflection, and knowledge of their own existence and of the past and the future. As we have seen, there is a basic problem here in that the relationship between physical characteristics and mental states is not readily analysed. Descartes for example posited the view that a person is a combination of two separate entities – the body and the mind. Only the mind is conscious. On this view (Cartesian dualism) it is perfectly conceivable, as Ayer (1963, p. 83) points out, that either could exist without the other, without in any way suggesting that it is

14

impossible for there to be any causal connection between them. And indeed, we may on occasion believe that an individual is physically present but that all consciousness is lost; that in some senses, the individual is no longer a person as we normally understand the concept. For example, it could be argued that a doctor's decision to turn off a life support machine depends upon the belief that, since there is no evidence of consciousness, the individual can no longer exist as a person. This is of course a moot point but what we are suggesting is that it is possible to conceive of consciousness as distinct from physical states.

Nevertheless, the thrust of much philosophical investigation has been to replace Descartes's *dualism* with some form of *monism*, i.e. to argue that far from there being an unbridgeable gap between the two, consciousness and the body have to be explained in terms which refer to the inextricable unity of mind and matter. Campbell (1975, p. 119) summarises this neatly in a way that is sufficient for our purposes when he argues 'Other (philosophical) systems either reduce the world of ideas to the world of things (Materialism) or find ultimate reality only in the world of ideas (Idealism).' Recent proponents of materialism have included Ryle (1973), and the materialist system can be identified in the empiricist philosophy of Hume.

Whatever the relationship is between consciousness and bodily status, the belief that persons are conscious beings entails a number of implications which will help us to advance our exploration of personhood. These are (i) individuals as persons have personal identity and (ii) individuals as persons are in some respects free.

(i) Personal identity. The capacity for self-reflection and self-awareness endows the individual human being with the ability to conceive of himself as a being independent of other beings. That is, quite simply, he can conceive of himself as a person. As a corollary of this, he can appreciate, without in any way having to prove it irrefutably, that there are other persons in the world and that his identification of his status as a person in some way associates him with others to whom he may then adopt particular relationships on this basis. As Strawson (quoted in Ayer, 1963, p. 86) suggests,

> It is a necessary condition of one's ascribing states of
> consciousness, experiences, to oneself in the way that one does,
> that one should also ascribe them or be prepared to ascribe
> them to others who are not oneself.

Though an individual may retain some form of personal identity, it is nevertheless tied up in some way with the existence of other persons.

A further feature is that the capacity for self-awareness, the possession of a personal identity, bestows on the individual a sense of continuity in time. That is, there is something about being a person which is enduring and not completely consonant with bodily changes, though the one may still of course have some implications for the other.

(ii) Consciousness and freedom. Being conscious of the world means that in some senses the individual is free from it. Though it does not itself negate the determinist thesis, the possession of consciousness, or to put it better, being conscious means that individuals can be aware of the constraints, internal or external, which may appear to limit their capacity for self-willed action. Indeed, some philosophers would go further and argue that the individual has the capacity to be totally free of all constraints since what the individual wishes to do is in the final analysis a decision for which he alone is responsible. The existentialists hold that each individual has the capacity to be totally responsible for the kind of person he turns out to be; even that is within the competence of individuals.

4 On becoming a person

We have already seen that, though there are various attributes which may be associated with being a person, such as rationality and consciousness, there are individuals whose status is somewhat ambiguous insofar as they may not wholly possess these characteristics. For example, children are often not considered to be capable of truly rational action; the mentally ill may not be considered fully rational persons; and prisoners, though rational, have partly lost the opportunity to exercise their will in accord with their reason. This brings us to an important point. The status of personhood cannot, as we have already anticipated, be inferred directly from a particular biological or physical endowment. A (biologically) human individual is not automatically a person. Rather, it has to be seen that personhood is socially defined and that no individual becomes a person without going through a social process of identification and ascription. The definitive attributes of personhood, which include rationality and consciousness, are only acquired through socialisation and their recognition as relevant attributes is necessarily a social process. We may add, therefore, to the list of attributes of the person discussed above, those that emphasise the social aspect of an individual's becoming a person. It will be seen that rationality and consciousness are themselves also very largely a social product.

Psychologically, the individual develops a personal identity only in the context of relationships with others. This is not to deny the importance of material conditions, heredity, the natural environment or many other factors but simply to recognise that relationships with significant others are crucially important in the development of normal human attributes. For argument's sake we may imagine a human creature reared in isolation from human contact. He could not conceivably be a person: he would not, in the ordinary meaning of the term, be socialised. Through socialisation the individual absorbs the culture in which he is brought up. In social work the study of human growth and behaviour has always been seen as centrally important to developing the understanding necessary for practice and in this field most attention has been given to those theorists – such as Freud, Bowlby, Erikson – who emphasise the essentially social aspect of the development of normal human attributes.

From the point of view of social interaction, the human being attains the status of personhood by virtue of his participation in the social structures which nurture him and which he contributes to. These include the family, community, workplace, etc. Personhood is conferred upon the individual by a social process which establishes who and what he is, and which grants recognition of his identity. Thus the development of individual personality is accompanied by the acquisition of social statuses and roles. Where an individual can clearly be said to possess, or not, the standard attributes there is not usually any difficulty in deciding whether he is a person. Problems arise in precisely those marginal cases where the generally accepted criteria of personhood fail to give an unambiguous answer as to whether someone is, or has been, or will become a person. A child of two may not possess full rationality, but is normally believed to be a person. Someone recently dead would seem to retain the status of personhood for a time, as evidenced by customs requiring respect for the dead, despite his manifestly lacking even sentience.

The interplay between psychological development and acquisition of the status of personhood contributes to the individual's sense of self. His conception of himself develops in response to his contact with other selves; it is socially engendered. He enters a world of relationships in which he is able to recognise and appreciate that there are other persons. He sees that as a group member he has reciprocal relationships with other persons in important respects not dissimilar from himself. Communication with others is essential to sustain this process.

We have referred to the standard attributes of personhood, but it is very important to grasp that the relevant criteria are culturally and historically contingent, and in fact are highly variable. Anthropologists have provided numerous examples which are markedly different from those that obtain in contemporary western societies.[4] Because the process of becoming a person involves a social definition, it is dependent upon prevailing conceptions of personhood and the social order as a whole. Consider for example the situation of the newborn infant in our society. It seems to be conventionally accepted that he automatically acquires personhood immediately upon being born. Some people would want to extend this backwards in time and include the unborn foetus. On the other hand the according of personhood to the newborn may well be a relatively recent phenomenon. The rituals of baptism seem to echo a time when full social status was not acquired until some days, or weeks, after the birth. To take another context, in cases involving newborn infants with major congenital defects it appears they are sometimes treated in ways which would be inconsistent with the status of personhood, notably in being allowed to starve to death (Gustafson, 1980).

A further complication of personhood is that it may be extended to non-humans, such as gods and spirits. Indeed several major religions incorporate the idea of a personal relationship with a purely abstract, non-material, non-corporeal deity. Moving from the exalted to dangerously near the banal, it is possible that personhood is extended to domestic pets. When people say their dog is one of the family they may be speaking more literally than metaphorically. The pet may well receive every possible care and comfort, denied to arguably more deserving persons away from the family orbit.

The concept of the person must, therefore, be seen as culturally and historically relative. There is however the danger that if this argument is extended too far it becomes impossible to entertain a meaningful dialogue on the subject; pressed too far, the whole edifice threatens to sink into a sea of relativism. Under such an attack all attempts to understand social reality can be written off as merely the product of particular cultural conditions; truth is neither here nor there, and the pursuit of guidelines for knowledge and action becomes hopeless and futile. We shall not get involved in arguments that offer an escape from this impasse.[5] However, in utilising a concept of the person we shall remain broadly in the western tradition. Our discussion of social work must therefore be interpreted in this light. There are theoretical as well as practical dangers involved in trying to take social work out of the social context of its origins (Midgley, 1981).

5 The moral status of persons

In this chapter we have proposed in effect that the concept of a person is derived from the attributes and properties generally associated with persons. The notion of a person entails the ideas of moral agency and responsibility. We have identified the attributes of rationality and consciousness as being of key importance in the understanding of what it is to be a person. We have made the point that becoming a person is essentially a social process. However we have also seen that none of these features of persons provide an infallible method of identifying who is, and what is not, a person. Various entities which seem to fail the tests of personhood nevertheless acquire it, and conversely many humans who seem to merit the status of persons are denied it. Watson (1980, pp. 59ff.) suggests that the idea of 'respect for persons' should be replaced by 'respect for human beings' as the moral basis for social policy, on the grounds that 'persons' defines the objects of respect too narrowly. However, the possession of personhood is not the same as the possession of its typical attributes, and to broaden the scope of the principle of respect to include all human beings merely takes us back to problematic cases, such as the foetus and the terminally comatose, already referred to. This leads then to the important point that personhood cannot simply be reduced to its typical signs; it is necessarily also a *moral* status, created by a process of social ascription. This means that those entities who are accorded the standing of personhood are seen to be entitled to certain kinds of treatment, even if their claim to the attributes of personhood may be dubious. It is in this light that the concept of respect for persons becomes almost tautologous as suggested above. Persons are, ipso facto, those entities to whom the moral principle of respect must be extended. A similar kind of apparent tautology is noticeable in colloquial expressions such as 'treating people as people' or 'treating clients as people'.

The alternative formulation of the concept, that every person should be treated as an end in himself, is useful for avoiding the danger of tautology. It is inherent in the concept of personhood advanced above that persons should be treated as *ends*, just as the idea of *respect* is inherent in that concept. If someone possesses the attributes of personhood he must, logically, respect other persons who by definition have similar attributes; non-respect for others would be logically incompatible with respect for himself, as it would destroy the basis for his own personhood (and incidentally the basis of his non-respect for others). This is similar to the principle of universality, according to which any plausible moral theory must apply the same standards to all. It is only by virtue of ourselves possessing similar attributes (especially rationality) to those which presumably command our respect in others that we are even able to appreciate the value of these attributes in ourselves and others. Inasmuch therefore as each person is an end for himself, he must treat others as ends. Downie and Telfer (1969) analyse various interpretations and difficulties of the idea of 'respect for persons as ends', and defend the idea of respect for persons as the 'supreme regulative principle'. Taking a similar line, Plant (1970) argues that respect for persons is a 'presupposition of morality'. Whatever terms the idea is stated in, it is very widely accepted both within and outside social work as the fundamental and irreducible principle. As Downie and Telfer remark, 'The idea of the individual person as of supreme worth is fundamental to the moral, political and religious ideas of our society' (1969, p. 9).

Our conclusion is thus that once an entity is established as the possessor of the moral status of personhood it is entitled to treatment on certain principles, even if its possession of the usual attributes of personhood is questionable or incomplete. In the next chapter we shall discuss how these principles might be given a practical interpretation by examining the rights of persons involved in social work. However, it is widely thought that there is more to respect for persons than just doing one's duty by them or treating them correctly. Downie and Telfer argue that respect for persons is an attitude as well as a principle of action, and invoke the idea of *agape*, a Greek term which can be understood to mean selfless or brotherly love, or charity in the archaic sense of the Authorised Version of the Bible. Campbell (1975) argues that respect for persons must combine reason and emotion. In these views the austere aspect of Kant's ethic of duty is softened by a humanistic concern which in our culture is most notably expressed in the Christian tradition. In the caring professions the identification of human concern with respect for persons has indeed been so widespread that it threatens to subvert the logic of the Kantian position. 'Kant does not say that action inspired by spontaneous love or sympathetic feeling has no value at all, but he does not think it has moral value' (Acton, 1970, p. 11); but Simpkin (1979, p. 99), writing as a practising social worker, seems to think that for social workers ' "respect" is only too often a cover for pity and even contempt'. This is a misunderstanding of respect for persons; true respect may not always by unpitying, but mere pity negates respect. Downie and Telfer's notion of *cherishing* much better expresses the combination of rational and emotional elements which respect entails.

Even though a combination of the ethic of duty with the ethic of love is philosophically problematic, it is an attractive avenue for the social worker and the caring professions generally. Experience teaches that a form of respect based too narrowly on duty leads to a stilted professional relationship; most social workers probably take for granted that, as a matter of empirical fact, it is impossible to show respect for persons in practice if a conception of the duties of the professional relationship is not animated by a genuine human and personal concern. The counselling literature repeatedly stresses the need for this concern. For practice which truly expresses respect to be based simply on philosophical arguments about duty seems implausible on psychological grounds. Social work cannot, of its nature, be practised without the caring and love which, perhaps, underlies received conceptions of professionally ethical behaviour.

Social workers spend a substantial amount of time dealing very directly with people who are anxious, confused, angry, ignorant, in want, dependent, or otherwise demanding. As in other caring professions, there are norms to protect the worker from engulfment. The worker is supposed to avoid getting over-involved emotionally with his clients. Some areas of the worker's life and personality are deemed beyond the parameters of relevance which define the content of the worker-client relationship. This professional distancing is perfectly understandable if we accept that the social worker needs to defend the boundaries of his own person, and to protect himself from excessive fatigue. Social workers also need to ensure that they will avoid exploiting their clients. They need, presumably, to remain detached enough to avoid their relationship with their client leading to any compromising situation, where they might be open to accusations of bias or a lack of objectivity. In the practice of social work these norms are transmitted as the appropriate models for students and new workers, and bolstered through supervision and the professional subculture. There is however a substantial danger that these norms lead to a negation of the attitude of respect for persons. The detachment which categorises clients to make them easier to deal with paves the way for treatment by category. This is readily seen in, for example, the workaday slang which refers to such things as 'sectioning' (sic) someone or 'doing a Part IV', much as doctors sometimes refer to their patients by the name of their medical condition. In a more extreme form it may lead to clients being, in effect, depersonalised; they are treated not as persons but as problems. Cynicism is the beginning of a scale which extends to misanthropy. Such an attitude may be accompanied and reinforced by a scientistic approach to human beings, as was suggested at the outset of this chapter.

It may be objected that to embrace the opposite attitude wholeheartedly, and reject the professional norms sketched above, would require an impossible and probably undesirable degree of saintliness and self-sacrifice. Overinvolvement by the professional could be seen as unduly intrusive, and might well be dangerous for the client. We do not wish to argue that professional distance is necessarily wrong, or dispensable. Nevertheless there is much in current practice to justify concern about a lack of authenticity in worker-client relationships. A number of writers[6] have suggested there exists a risk that the social worker's genuine concern for his client as a fellow human being will be rendered impossible to express, or even be extinguished, by the exigencies of an occupational role practised largely from state bureaucracies and emphasising technical efficiency at the expense of personal sharing.

It is probably true that need for the love of social workers will usually exceed the strength of most of them to respond to it. But social workers after all are not alone in having to cope with a world where most personal contacts can never reach the level of personal relationships. We might still look for the possibility of enabling that gift at least in some instances. The social worker should be prepared sometimes to go beyond the confines of the conventionalised professional relationship, where these threaten to stultify its authenticity. This may occur much more commonly and readily than a reading of many textbooks would lead one to suppose. Halmos (1978a, p. 77) presented a powerful case that the merely objective, scientific attitude does not in fact adequately characterise professional counselling relationships: 'The counsellors . . . consider their warm personal attachment to the help seeker as a vital instrument of helping.' To transcend professional relationships needs daring, imagination, and trust; but to do so it may sometimes be necessary to give full recognition to the moral status of persons.

Chapter two

Rights, self-determination, paternalism and authority

1 Rights and duties in social work

In this chapter we shall consider how the conception of the person discussed in the last chapter can be translated into a basis for action in social work. We shall do so through the medium of rights. The point of formulating and defending conceptions of rights is that doing so clarifies what are the legitimate expectations of the various actors in a given type of situation. Together with the related concept of duty, this approach helps to establish what one ought to do and expect others to do, in practical terms. Rights and duties may be thought of, therefore, as a way of expressing the expectations implicit in social and moral values in an operational form. By implication, the dialogue on rights reveals areas of agreement or disagreement in the determination of basic values and their inter-pretation. We will consider first the nature of rights and duties in general terms, and move from there to ask what rights and duties are involved in social work. More specifically we will consider the client's putative right of self-determination and the worker's puta-tive right of intervention. These questions will lead respectively to an evaluation of responsibility and freedom, and self-determination. Finally, we will examine authority in social work in the light of the preceding considerations.

If the idea of rights initially suggests a certain appealing clarity, this fades quickly once we begin to consider its content in detail. Rights may be categorised as natural, human, legal, moral, social, civil, economic, welfare . . . and much else besides. We will approach the topic by proposing a number of dichotomous distinc-tions which enable one to build up a classification of rights. As we shall be using a total of five dichotomies that are mostly logically independent, the classification we present cannot conveniently be represented as a whole on a single two-dimensional diagram. We

23

shall therefore supplement the discussion with a number of two-dimensional diagrams which illustrate some significant aspects of the classification.

The first distinction is between *universal* and *particular* rights. A universal right applies to everybody without exception; a particular right applies to a limited class of persons, or even a single person.

The second distinction is between *absolute* (or unqualified) and *qualified* (or conditional) rights. An absolute right is always valid; there are absolutely no circumstances under which it does not obtain. But a qualified right may rightfully be suspended in certain circumstances.

If we combine these two dimensions we have the scheme in Figure 1.

	Universal	Particular
Absolute	1	2
Qualified	3	4

Fig. 1 Rights

Examining each cell in turn we may classify certain rights. (1) There seem to be very few absolute universal rights by this (admittedly stringent) definition. The concept of respect for persons may be said logically to necessitate the recognition of an absolute universal right to be treated as an end and not simply as a means. This is clearly of great importance; and it is difficult to think of any other right in the same class which would be generally accepted. (2) Absolute particular rights apply without qualification to everyone in a certain category. For example, all parents living in Britain have an absolute right to claim Child Benefit.[1] (3) Qualified universal rights apply to everybody, except that they may also be withdrawn from anybody as a result of the application of criteria which apply to all. Such a withdrawal of rights might for example arise as a result of the person being found guilty of a crime. By far the most important of the qualified universal rights are those usually known as natural or human rights. The idea of natural rights – that is, rights deducible simply from the natural characteristics of mankind – may seem somewhat puzzling and arbitrary to the twentieth-century mind, accustomed to notions of the cultural and temporal relativity of man's view of himself. On the other hand the doctrine of human rights has an undeniable contemporary appeal and seems altogether more intelligible. For all that, the content of human rights derives from the natural rights tradition and they can be treated as near enough the same thing. A useful statement of the generally accepted human rights is contained in the United Nations Universal Declaration of Human Rights (UN, 1948) but this also contains a good many provisions which may not be justified as human rights.

Human rights must be regarded as qualified because there are generally recognised grounds for withholding them. The right to liberty is suspended for the imprisoned criminal; the right to free speech is restricted by wartime censorship; the right of habeas corpus is suspended in emergencies, etc.

(4) Qualified particular rights are those which may apply to certain persons under certain conditions. For example, I have a (legal) right to overtime pay if I have worked overtime and if I have a contract of employment which provides for overtime pay to be paid. Similarly, I have a right to a pension if I am over the prescribed retirement age and I have satisfied the necessary contribution conditions. It should be clear why qualified particular rights are the ones which in practice create most of the difficulties of interpretation and application; both the grounds for qualifying for the right, and the grounds for treating someone as being covered or not, are liable to dispute. In social welfare generally and in social work in particular, the most important debates and difficulties centre on qualified particular rights; we are concerned with things like welfare rights and rights to discretionary services such as social work and some forms of medical care.

The next two dichotomies may also be conveniently treated as a pair. *Moral* rights stem from the recognition that one is a person, or a person in a given sort of situation. (An argument of the same general form is used by some to extend rights to animals and other non-persons.) *Legal* rights are created by legislation, or are evolved by tradition in those systems that recognise common law or its equivalent. Legal rights may be classified as *positive* or *nominal*. A positive right is one that is not only recognised as such, but for which there actually exist effective means of implementation. Nominal rights exist in law but are unavailable for various practical reasons to some or all of those who are entitled to them.

These dichotomies may again be combined, but as they are not independent the relationship differs from Figure 1. From the preceding definitions we arrive at Figure 2.

Several comments may be made at this point. (i) Some philosophers have argued that there can be no such things as nominal rights: only positive rights which are actually enforceable are worth calling rights. This view eliminates as invalid all the remaining categories in Figure 2.

(ii) The scheme above assumes that all positive rights are also legal rights. This is a reasonably good approximation for western

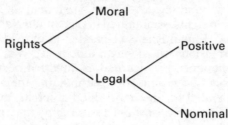

Fig. 2

societies but might well be invalid in the context of, for example, a primitive society without formal legal systems but possessing effective mechanisms for protecting rights.

(iii) The distinction between moral and legal rights is logical rather than necessarily one of content. Thus the right we may claim to free speech may be both moral and legal. The fact that the substance of a right may be both moral and legal does not however invalidate the logical distinction between the two.

(iv) A full statement of moral rights may be equivalent to a moral system; but any moral system which calls for the recognition of more than simply the rights and duties of individuals would only be partially described by a theory of rights. Most religions come into this category. More practically, and to avoid circularity, we can say that holding a certain moral position logically necessitates the recognition of certain moral rights, and then we can examine conduct to see whether these moral rights are being respected.

(v) The distinction between positive and nominal rights is of considerable practical importance. For example, I have a nominal legal right to educate my children privately if the law allows it; but for this to be a positive right I would need in addition to have sufficient money to pay for it, for there to be a school available of acceptable quality, and so forth. Similar arguments apply to private medical treatment and many other kinds of provision.

The four dichotomies proposed so far do not operate in isolation from each other; they intersect, giving a relatively large number (12) of different kinds of rights. We do not intend to examine all the ramifications of this scheme, but we shall draw attention to some additional features of interest.

Qualified universal rights, which we have already identified with human rights, may be moral, legal, or both. Human rights are justifiable on moral grounds, but they may or may not also exist as legal rights for the citizens of any given state at a given time. The rights to choose one's government, of free speech, of association, of equality before the law, are all examples of human rights which are also legal rights in many countries. Of course there also exist countries where some of these legal rights are purely nominal and not positive.

The proper extent of human rights is a much debated question. Cranston (1967) has argued that whereas, for example, no one would deny that the right to life is a universal human right, to stretch the idea to include such things as social security goes so far beyond the meaning of the term that the point of a concept of human rights is lost. In the light of the distinctions we have proposed, it could be argued that some of the more doubtful items, such as holidays with pay (Article 24 of the UN Declaration) should be regarded as qualified particular legal rights, and thus quite distinct from the central human rights, such as freedom, which ought to be regarded as qualified, universal, and preferably to exist as legal and positive rights.

The government's pursuit of morally unjust policies may be held to give me, as a citizen adversely affected by them, the right to perform acts of civil disobedience such as non-payment of taxes; but others might claim that I have an over-riding duty to obey the law. We shall consider this problem in Chapter 4. If civil disobedience is defined as a principled breaking of the law on moral grounds, it is obviously illegal; but it is also possible for civil disobedience to consist of a legally valid response to the government's own illegal behaviour.

The rights that require specific elucidation for successful application in social work are mostly qualified particular rights and will be discussed in later sections of this chapter. The application of universal rights cannot, without absurdity, be essentially different in social work from any other context, although it may be that the social work context raises difficulties which are intrinsically worth examining. Some of the difficulties associated with the recognition of these elusive and perhaps insecure rights are well portrayed by T.D. Campbell's (1978) suggestion and analysis of 'discretionary rights'. Campbell contrasts the clear-cut legal idea implicit in a 'right' to welfare state services with the much less clearly defined individualised care, informed by professional judgement, which social workers primarily see themselves as providing. Nonetheless social workers are agents of the state for the provision of a welfare service, and perhaps ought therefore to be subject to the same legal controls as other branches of the executive if the exercise of their professional judgement and professional power is not to result in arbitrariness and injustice. The idea of a discretionary right is advanced to bridge the rights of the client with the professional power of the social worker. Campbell acknowledges the possibility that the idea of discretionary rights may be self-contradictory; but if discretionary rights are identified as a type of qualified particular

27

right this danger can be avoided. Our procedure will be to take a cautious and conventional view of the extent of qualified universal rights and postulate that they are no more problematic for social workers than anyone else. Doubtful cases, such as the supposed right to self-determination, will be treated initially as qualified particular rights. If on analysis their scope turns out to be larger than first assumed, one might then take the view that they could be serious candidates for the status of qualified universal rights. We shall be concerned principally with moral rather than legal rights, as this is not intended to be a legal textbook; but the conflict of known legal rights with moral rights will arise from time to time.

Rights are usually said to entail duties, but there are differing views on the strictness of this correlation. The most straightforward analysis is that every right which a person has must logically imply a duty on someone else's part to fulfil the right.[2] If you have a duty to pay me what you owe me, I have a right to the money. There are, however, a number of problems with this conception. If I have a duty to perform an action, there is a certain sense in which I must also have the right to perform it, or otherwise my position would be absurd. We might say in a social work context that it would be absurd to place a duty on a social worker to investigate an allegation of cruelty to a child without also giving him a right to do so. By contrast, I may have a right without a duty; for instance I have a legal right to vote in the election, but not (in Britain) a legal duty to do so. This suggests that the relationship between rights and duties is not a simple bilaterally symmetrical one. We might also note that, for example, the UN Declaration provides for a number of 'rights' and 'freedoms', such as the right to life and the freedom from torture. Although they are lumped together in the Declaration it seems probable that they are not strictly comparable. One response to this problem is to adopt the distinction proposed by Raphael (1967, 1976) between rights of action and rights of recipience. A right of action is a liberty or absence of obligation; it is a freedom *to* do something. On the other hand a right of recipience is a right against someone to receive something, or claim right. The freedom *from* something is also a right of recipience, in that it is a claim against everyone else not to have imposed whatever it is that a freedom from is being claimed, e.g. enslavement.

The distinction between rights of action and recipience makes possible a clearer view of the relation between rights and duties. A right of recipience logically requires a corresponding duty on the other side. On the other hand a right of action lays no specific duty on anyone. The social worker who hears an allegation of child abuse may arguably have a right of action to investigate it; this implies no duty. If it is held that the child has a right of recipience to protection from abuse, then the social worker may also have a duty of intervention. But the social worker's right of recipience, if it exists, may also or alternatively imply his right of recipience to take remedial action against those responsible for the abuse. Such a right of recipience would consist of an entitlement to non-interference from others in his pursuit of remedial action. Now the entitlements that derive from the social worker's rights of action and recipience are dissimilar, and it will be important therefore to clarify whether such rights are rights of action or recipience.

2 The client

The list of clients' rights that one might arrive at on a perusal of the social work literature is fairly short. A typical list might comprise the following:

    (i) to be treated as an end;

   (ii) to self-determination;

  (iii) to be accepted for what one is, and not encounter an attitude of condemnation;

  (iv) to be treated as a unique individual and not merely as belonging to a certain category;

   (v) to non-discrimination on irrelevant grounds, such as race;

  (vi) to treatment on the principles of honesty, openness and non-deception;

 (vii) to have information given to the worker in the course of social work treatment treated as confidential;

(viii) to a professionally competent service;

  (ix) to access to resources for which there exists an entitlement ('welfare rights').

If this is accepted as a reasonably representative list, the first question to ask about it is, perhaps, where such rights come from, or how they may be justified. It is less than satisfactory to invoke rights without being able to give a basis for them. The first six items at least are best regarded as direct amplifications or derivations of the principle of respect for persons, which we have discussed in the previous chapter. They derive therefore from a particular conception of the person and of moral agency; and, while we have seen that this conception is by no means without its theoretical difficulties and ambiguities, it provides a fairly clear and widely accepted reference point. A second source of justification for these rights may be sought in those general theories that aim to define the nature and extent of moral obligation. These will be reviewed in the next chapter. Thirdly, we may refer to a conception of the ethical implications of taking on a professional role, which itself owes much to the political ideology of liberalism. These topics will be addressed in the final two chapters.

The limitations upon the client's ability to exercise the rights listed above may initially be divided into two classes, theoretical and practical. In this section we shall briefly survey the nature of these limitations in general terms, and then consider the case of self-determination in more detail. Theoretical limitations are inferred a priori from the nature and basis of the right, while practical limitations result from imperfections of the world. Three sorts of theoretical limitations may be noted: those that make a right qualified, those that make it particular, and thirdly the possibility that a so-called right may be incoherent or meaningless.

We have identified a number of the rights in question as derivative from the concept of respect for persons. Insofar as this is true, the following remarks apply: because this principle must necessarily represent what we have called a universal right (because respect for persons is only meaningful if it refers to *all* persons), it does not serve to identify what rights appertain to clients as clients. We must simply say that clienthood is not in itself a relevant consideration in deciding the content or scope of the rights that derive from respect for persons. This formal conclusion does not, of course, obviate the necessity of trying to decide how to implement the rights required by respect for persons, and therefore some requirements on social work.

Respect for persons implies, as we have just remarked, the absolute universal right to be treated as an end. Probably it is the only such right. But much debate on the ethics of social work stems from the recognition that the derivative or cognate principles are not necessarily either absolute or universal. We shall sketch the grounds for restricting the range of persons to whom the rights apply (in what respects are they justifiably particular?) and the conditions under which they may be justifiably restricted (why qualified?). In general terms the rights derivative from respect for persons are particular in that they may be held to be inapplicable to the following cases:

(a)　the mentally incompetent, including the severely mentally ill or handicapped, the demented, etc.;
(b)　children below a certain age or mental capacity;
(c)　those judged to lack the capacity for moral action, e.g. those with certain psychopathic conditions.

Obviously these classes present a series of extremely vexatious boundary problems. Just how mentally incompetent, for example, must someone be before he is deemed incapable of being treated as a normal person?

The rights derivative of respect for persons are qualified in that arguably they may rightfully be denied in the following circumstances:

(a)   where the interests of others are adversely affected to an unacceptable degree;
(b)   where there is a persistent wilful refusal to act morally;
(c)   where the person's actions break the law;
(d)   where the person's actions will damage his own interests.

The right of self-determination provides a specially pertinent case of the significance of these limitations. Self-determination, or self-direction, has probably received far more discussion in the literature of social work ethics than any other single topic. It expresses a powerful intuition: that social workers should stimulate and enhance the client's capacity for making his own decisions and living his own life by his own standards. Social workers should not deceive or propel the client into a course of action that runs contrary to his true wishes. The justification for this principle is basically twofold. Firstly, self-determination is an ethical requirement: to breach it negates the principle of respect for persons. Secondly, as a matter of practical observation, manipulative, deceitful or coercive intervention is unlikely to be effective in the long run. However, as the literature and everyday experience testify, the principle is impossible to apply in an absolute form. As we remarked above, the right of self-determination is both particular and qualified. The problem is deciding on where the limits should fall.

The assumption of parental rights by social workers on behalf of their employing authority provides an interesting case of the problems of interpreting how to apply the principle of self-determination. Let us suppose that the parent whose rights are being abrogated is not mentally incompetent or otherwise ineligible to exercise self-determination; and further that there are reasonable grounds for believing that the child in question may be in danger from his parent's actions or want of satisfactory actions. We might then argue that the danger to the child justifies interfering with the parent's presumptive right to care for the child. We might further argue that the child's self-determination, so far as he may be presumed to have the capacity or potential for it, should be protected even at the cost of reducing the parent's. On the other hand, given that the parent has the capacity for moral action, it would seem to run counter to the principle of self-determination to take the drastic step of reducing the area in which he may exercise it by removing the child. Arguments like these can be multiplied almost indefinitely, and tend perhaps towards the conclusion that the concept of a right of self-determination is really of no use in resolving the dilemmas of practice; but if that is true, it is paradoxical that self-determination should be given such a prominent place in social work ethics.

There is, and can be, no final answer to these questions. The definition of someone as too mentally incompetent, immature or deluded to exercise true self-determination is a social process which takes place in a given cultural and historical context. It depends upon, and reflects, a specific conception of what constitutes an adequate mental competence; we need only recall, say, the treatment of witches in medieval Europe, or of dissidents in some contemporary totalitarian regimes, to find examples of conceptions which would be totally unacceptable in social work. Similarly, the extent to which a person's exercise of self-determination can be allowed to intrude upon the interests of himself or others, or upon the demands of law and morality, is a historically and culturally contingent matter.

Recognising the social and historical relativity of these problems is cold comfort for the social worker, who must still try to make up his own mind in specific cases. We suggest, however, that for the most part social workers are content, rightly or wrongly, to adopt conventional norms and wisdoms. Where clear standards are not readily available, they are built up over time as a sediment of practice within social work agencies. This process establishes the relationship between the self-determination which social workers aspire to promote and the social control which, however reluctantly, they admit as a consequence or an end of social work. Social workers act as agents of social control by defining the area within which self-determination is to be allowed; that is, in precisely what respects the right is particular and qualified.

The third limitation on clients' rights which may be inferred on theoretical grounds arises if it is held that the alleged right is incoherent, illusory or meaningless. There are various instances of this, including the following. Acceptance and individualisation may be held to be psychologically impossible for the worker to put into practice when confronted by an individual he finds repugnant. Honesty may be held to be impossible in principle if we remember that the client-worker relationship is inevitably constrained within the boundaries of certain expectations on either side, not all of which are reciprocal. Absolute confidentiality, in the sense that nothing whatever that passed between worker and client would be communicated to anyone else without the client's explicit consent, is meaningless in the context of social work practised from large bureaucracies. If we are to invoke rights, we must be able to show that the rights in question are in principle attainable, and not ruled out because they conflict with logic or empirical fact.

Self-determination, once again, presents a difficult problem of meaningfulness. The capacity for self-determination is presumably based on the person's ability to make choices that will govern the course of his life in some way; the assumption must be that at least in certain respects a person's behaviour is subject to his will. It depends therefore on a libertarian conception of human nature. However, as we saw in the previous chapter, the determinist thesis is powerful in social work as elsewhere. If one holds a strongly deterministic view of human action it is extremely difficult to give credence to the possibility of self-determination: one contradicts the other.

Even if we reject determinism, what self-determination actually requires we should do in practical situations is still fairly obscure. Perhaps the leading idea is that a commitment to self-determination should serve to enhance a person's freedom and his capacity to pursue and realise his own goals. We soon find, however, that arriving at a specification of those goals is not a simple matter. What should be done if a person defines his goals on the basis of inadequate or wrong information? Or if his estimates of what is desirable are based on insufficient opportunity for educated appraisal? Berlin's (1969) concept of negative freedom, which emphasises freedom *from* undue interference, is apt to seem a poor substitute for the vision of a more fulfilled life which the social worker may wish his clients to pursue. The notion of positive freedom – freedom *to* be one's own master – underlies much social reformism, whether focused on the individual or the larger community. We shall return to this shortly in the context of paternalism.

The right to a professionally competent service is obviously a particular right of clients, but is presumably absolute in that all clients have such a right. On the other hand, rights to the service as such, or to a certain type of service, along with rights to other resources for which there may exist an entitlement such as certain welfare benefits, are notoriously difficult to pin down satisfactorily. This leads us from the theoretical limitations on rights discussed above to the question of practical limitations that are particularly significant in instances of this sort, which we shall refer to as resource rights.

Take, for example, the situation of a mentally handicapped person living in the community. It might readily be agreed that he had rights to a range of facilities and services that enabled him to live a life approximating to that of a normal person in the same community. These might include the opportunity of work appropriate to his talents and capacities, a fair income, some form of sheltered housing that enabled him to lead his own life without unwanted or excessive dependence on parents or others, and the opportunity to marry and possibly to have children. Now it will not be disputed that the living situation of many mentally handicapped people falls far short of these ideals. The issue here is that although we may agree that the person possesses valid rights of the kinds indicated, factors such as non-availability of resources, lack of professional skill and imagination, or lack of political motivation to address the problem may prevent the realisation of these rights. This state of affairs is in a way more worrying than when rights are unattainable on theoretical grounds, because it implies the existence of a remediable injustice; it calls out for practical action, and the price of non-response may be a forfeiture of the integrity of the social work enterprise.

If we leave aside the area of human rights, resource rights specific to the context of social work are nearly all qualified and particular. Examples in addition to those already mentioned include rights to residential care for the elderly infirm, sheltered accommodation, day care for young children, discretionary financial aid, practicel aids and adaptations, intermediate treatment, child guidance, etc. But even if we agreed upon some ideal set of resource rights for clients according to category, it would plainly be impossible to implement them for all the relevant people simultaneously. The practical limitations on realising resource rights due to scarcety or maldistribution therefore generate a new set of theoretical problems.

The question of resource distribution, and hence of the meaning and validity of such things as welfare rights, cannot simply be resolved by appealing to a conception of the person or the client. The idea of rights, therefore, will not by itself enable us to decide how clients should be treated. Rather, the question of rights raises the problem of distributive justice, which we shall take up in Chapter 3.

Before leaving consideration of the client, it is worth asking what his duties may be, towards the social worker and towards others who figure in the social work involvement. In general it would seem that his duties to the social worker are relatively circumscribed. While social workers would no doubt prefer to be treated by their clients on the same sort of principles that they themselves undertake to show by their actions towards their clients, social workers must also be prepared to forgo such respect in many cases. The very nature of the client's predicament may make it unreasonable to expect him to adhere consistently to comparable standards and social workers cannot refuse to work with someone because of that. For example, a residential social worker cannot refuse to work with a difficult youngster because he is violent or abusive towards the worker, or steals from him. This lack of comparability of clients' and workers' duties underlines the difference between the respective role expectations in the client-worker relationship, and how different it is from ordinary friendship or ordinary relations between citizens, from which we expect a much higher degree of symmetry. The one duty which the client may owe the worker in nearly all cases is that he should enter into the transaction in good faith and not with an undeclared ulterior motive; he should not deliberately deceive. Even this requirement may be too stringent if the client is temporarily unable to do so because his problems prevent him from observing usual standards of honesty.

There has been increasing interest in having clients participate in the helping process with clearly formulated aims and responsibilities. This is sometimes expressed, in somewhat over-dignified language, as a 'contract' between client and worker. In such cases the client presumably has a duty to fulfil the terms of the working agreement reached with the worker. Various practical advantages of using clear working agreements – such as reducing anxiety and uncertainty, encouraging the client to take responsibility, and expediting treatment – have been identified in the literature. A working agreement may, however, be a coercive instrument in the hands of the worker when we remember the differences in power between worker and client. There is a danger, therefore, that working agreements could actually be used to reduce rather than enhance the client's rights and place upon him duties which are unfair or unrealistic.

The client's duties do not, of course, end with his obligation to the social worker. Indeed, the functions of social work are such that it is very often centrally concerned with the client's duties to his family and other members of society. The probationer has defaulted on part of his duty to society: the social worker is charged with ensuring that he makes reparations for this default. The social worker may have to deal with the relatives of homeless people, or with someone seeking residential care for an elderly relative. One possible and fairly common response (Bailey, 1980) is for the worker to ask that the relatives themselves shelter the homeless, or look after the elderly relative, rather than arranging alternative provision through state services. In other words, the worker cannot avoid expressing a practical morality and an ideology in addressing situations of this sort, as every possible response is value-laden.

3 The social worker

Is social work intervention a right or a duty of the worker? This apparently simple question masks a number of problematic issues both for social workers themselves and for those who employ or sponsor them. We shall approach the problem by asking to whom and by whom such a right or a duty may be owed, and what kind of right or duty may be involved.

(i) The social worker has a duty to his client to render an appropriate professional service. In this instance we take it that the legitimacy of the client's status as a client is not in doubt. The everyday situation would be where the client has requested the service and the worker agreed that he will provide it. The reciprocal relationship is that the client has a number of rights of recipience against the worker. These rights are identical to those discussed in the previous section. As well as requiring certain actions from the social worker, this relationship also requires him to refrain from certain actions.

(ii) The social worker may be held to have duties to third parties, i.e. persons other than himself or the client, or perhaps to society as a whole. Here the third parties have rights of recipience against the social worker requiring him to act, or refrain from acting, in certain ways.

This relationship arises from the fact that the social worker-client interaction does not take place in a social vacuum but is embedded in a matrix of social relationships. Social workers are expected to balance their commitment to their clients' interests with due regard for others in the situation. For example, the residential worker has to weigh the needs of one particular resident against those of other residents and the living group as a whole. Regard for third parties is further extended by the expectation that social workers should act as agents of the wider society under certain conditions. This expectation is clearly visible in the statutory duties that are laid upon social workers, as for example in arranging adoptions or supervising offenders on probation, and is implicit in the general social control function of social work. In examining the duties of the social worker in any given instance, it is worth asking to whom he is seen as accountable, and for what; in general we can expect that the range of duties will be diverse, and there will be a large number of persons to whom they are owed.

The first two cases show, then, that social workers in certain circumstances have a duty to intervene and that once a legitimate intervention has been established there are duties inherent in it. In the next three cases we proceed to the right of intervention.

(iii) Social workers can justifiably claim rights of recipience to be treated in certain ways with respect to the interests of some individuals other than their clients, and those non-clients will have a duty of cooperation or at least non-obstruction. Such rights are derived from the worker's commitment to his client's interests. The worker who acts as his client's agent in pressing for something his client needs can reasonably claim a right to be attended to with at least the same consideration that the client himself is entitled to. In fact, of course, a person may turn to a social worker in the hope or expectation that the worker will be more effective in realising the client's wishes than the client himself has been. So-called welfare rights work is an important example of this type of situation. It also arises when the worker acts as the client's agent in cases where the client is presumed to lack full competence, as with children, the mentally disordered, or the socially inept.

An important and difficult class of interventions is that in which the worker claims a right of recipience to intervene in a manner contrary to the client's wishes. When an intervention is against the client's wishes but conducted in what are believed to be his own interests, it may be described as paternalistic. (Acting contrary to both the client's wishes and interests could hardly be called social work.) It is precisely because social work is so often concerned with people who are deemed incapable of determining or pursuing their own best interests that paternalistic intervention presents such an important question: when, for example, a social worker is instrumental in committing a child offender to 'compulsory measures of care', it is done at least in the hope that this course best serves the child's interests.

It is doubtful whether the client in this case can be said to owe a duty which corresponds to the worker's right of recipience, because the intervention is undertaken precisely with the assumption that the client is incapable of fulfilling the normal criteria of competence and responsibility. The client here is presumed incapable of undertaking the relevant type of duty. A worker's right of paternalistic intervention must therefore be seen as a right of recipience against non-clients. The worker has a right to cooperation or non-obstruction from non-clients. Paternalistic intervention cannot be a right of recipience against the client himself.

(iv) It might be objected that the previous case denotes the worker's rights where the intervention is capable of legitimation on specific grounds other than those of some general right of intervention. A right of intervention in this latter sense would be a right of action, which lays no specific obligations on anyone else. The existence of such a right is implicitly and perhaps explicitly assumed in those cases where the worker takes the responsibility for initiating a piece of work in advance of, or in the absence of, any specific request from those whom the intervention is intended to benefit. In neighbourhood community work, for example, it is common for the worker and the agency to initiate a new project or activity without a substantial mandate from the population affected, in the hope that

37

they will be successful in persuading that population that the project merits their support. Such intervention requires more than a post hoc demonstration that the project was supported to show that it was ethically justified. For a source of justification we must turn to broader political theories and show, for example, that the intervention served a conception of social justice, or some other higher end. This will be considered in the next chapter.

(v) Having established that social workers' putative rights of intervention may, in different cases, reasonably be described either as rights of action or rights of recipience, we are faced with the somewhat paradoxical fact that social workers may also claim the right *not* to intervene. Social workers have gone on strike, refusing to perform their normal duties. This has certainly occasioned a great deal of heart-searching, not least because it leaves the social workers open to the accusation that they are worsening the plight of the weak and vulnerable in pursuit of their own narrow self-interest. It may be held that while social workers have a perfectly good legal right to strike, they lack a moral right to do so in the circumstances of what would, in other contexts, be an ordinary industrial dispute. Another type of right to non-intervention may arise when workers or their agencies claim that they may justifiably decline or give low priority to certain work which is agreed to fall, potentially, within their remit. It seems to be generally accepted, for example, that social work area teams should give lower priority to the elderly infirm than children at risk (DHSS, 1978).

A sceptic might feel that in claiming rights to both intervention and non-intervention in cases which are perfectly similar as regards the client, the social work profession is relinquishing any credible basis for claiming that social work is built on sound moral principles at all. The analysis of rights is, by itself, insufficient to answer this question: we must go on to examine the basis of moral action, and the relationship of ethical propositions to principles for practice.

4 Self-determination, paternalism and social control

In (iv) above we stated as one of the social worker's putative rights the right of intervention without the client's consent, and identified this as paternalistic. The popular image of paternalism is unfavourable: to label an action or policy as paternalist is often intended to be derogatory, and evokes images of misguided and patronising moralism, one's betters knowing what was good for one, and suffocating charity.[3] Paternalism is a central problem of liberal theory because it challenges the presumption that the individual is the best judge of his own welfare, and sets the problem of identifying some of the limits on freedom. However the view that paternalism is all bad will not withstand scrutiny. The notion derives from the actions a parent will take against his child's wishes but in his interests; no one disputes that the toddler must be prevented from putting his hand in the fire however much he might dislike being restrained. The problem of paternalism is essentially to locate its justifiable extent.

The social worker may wish to claim either or both of two sources of justification for a paternalistic intervention. In the first place he may be acting on behalf of the state when he implements paternalistic legislation which requires him to constrain his client's freedom in what is purportedly the client's own interest. Thus a young offender on a supervision order may be required to participate in some kind of treatment programme. An elderly person living alone and incapable of looking after himself adequately may be compulsorily removed from his home on the grounds that it is in his interests. On the other hand, the social worker may wish to act paternalistically not in response to legislation but as a matter of professional judgement on the basis of his special knowledge. He may believe that he knows his client's interests better than the client does and justify curtailing the client's freedom in order to promote those interests. This loss of freedom may be overt and recognised by all involved, but in other instances the worker may intentionally reduce the client's freedom by withholding material information or deliberately distorting the client's understanding of the situation. A client with hopelessly unrealistic aspirations may be led to accept a more realistic aim if his estimate of probabilities is manipulated by the worker.

Social workers are also involved in courses of action which may seem paternalistic, but are not. Arranging for someone's rent or fuel to be paid directly from his welfare income, instead of the money passing through his own hands with a risk of default, is not paternalistic if the client has given full consent and has not been misled as to the implications of the various courses open to him, or otherwise coerced. On the other hand, payments made in kind, such as clothing, furniture or food, when the client would prefer cash, do certainly limit the client's freedom when compared with cash payments and are therefore paternalistic in character. This does not necessarily mean that they are unjustifiable; they raise a particular instance of the general issue of the extent of justifiable paternalism.

It should now be apparent that self-determination, social control and paternalism have a complementary relation to each other. Social work places a very high value on promoting client self-determination, but no such right is tenable in an absolute form. It is bounded on one side by the regard which social workers must have of the interests of parties other than the client: thus social work acts as a force for social control,[4] by regulating the permissible extent of client self-determination. The right of self-determination is bounded on the other side by the regard which social workers must have of the interests of the client even if they are contradicted by his wishes: self-determination meets a border with justified paternalism. Consideration of this relationship sheds some light on why social work exhibits such confusion and ambivalence about the three elements of self-determination, paternalism and social control. The commitment to self-determination is strongly held, and yet at the same time social workers are bound, perhaps with some reluctance, to recognise the inevitable fact that some social work activities are designed to procure social control, and some represent acts of paternalism. Social workers perhaps sense that in a way they are expected to be on both sides of self-determination-social control and self-determination-paternalism boundaries at the same time. In each individual case some decision has to be made, or paralysis ensues; but without general principles for locating these boundaries, the decisions made are apt to be arbitrary, which is disorienting for the worker and quite possibly unjust in its impact on those who pay for and those who receive social work. Once again, the analysis of rights is, by itself, insufficient to decide where these boundaries of acceptable social control and justifiable paternalism should lie; these questions require a larger moral and political theory for their resolution.

5 Responsibility, authority and power

In this section we return to the theme of rights and duties in social work to discuss an important group of related concepts: accountability, responsibility, authority, and power. A social worker owes various duties to his client and other parties: we say that he is, or ought to be, accountable for his work. He is also expected to exercise authority: what is its source and justification? We are concerned therefore with the complex characteristic web of rights and duties that defines social work; clarifying this would go some way to locating its peculiar and difficult social position.

The notions of accountability and responsibility cover several questions, the distinctions between which are unfortunately apt to be lost if their associated prepositions are overlooked or omitted. (Although responsibility and accountability are sometimes distinguished and given narrower meanings than those adopted here, we shall follow conventional usage and treat them as synonymous unless qualified.) A social worker is responsible to someone for something. These two senses are at the same time distinct and complementary, as responsibility to and responsibility for cannot be described except in relation to each other. Responsibility, in its literal meaning of answerability, clearly requires someone to be responsible to; and responsibility to someone can be given no content unless we say what it is responsibility for. There is a further, third sense in which we speak of someone as being a responsible person, or acting responsibly: its negative is irresponsibility whereas the negative of the first two senses is non-responsibility.

The questions of to whom the social worker is responsible, and for what, are intrinsically complex. Undoubtedly the worker has responsibility with respect to his client, correlating with the duties discussed above. He will usually be accountable also to his superiors or managers, who will regulate the content and intent of his work to a greater or lesser extent. Indeed social workers may feel aggrieved if their work is structured by bureaucratic demands in a way that reduces the responsibility they take for it. He may be expected to show further accountability to the funding body which pays for the work, be it central or local government or a voluntary organisation. Besides, he may be required to comply with the expectations or policies of his professional association and trade union. Thus conflicts of responsibilities can easily arise. Should a worker accept an instruction from his trade union which would prejudice the service he believed he owed his clients? Should social workers divulge confidential information about individual clients to the governing body of the agency? More broadly still, the social worker is commonly held to have responsibilities to society as a whole, such as to care for the vulnerable, to protect the community from some of the consequences of deviant behaviour, and also to contribute to the political process of bringing about changes necessary to alleviate the social problems which the social worker confronts. Even stated so elliptically, this is a staggering list of responsibilities. How can it be manageable?

The problem of the feasibility of carrying out one's responsibilities in social work demands at least two separate lines of enquiry. In the first place one needs a moral and political theory to enable one to deal with conflicts of valid responsibilities such as those just mentioned. There is no a priori method of deciding, say, that one's responsibility to one's clients outweighs one's responsibility to one's employer: different cases require different decisions, and not all workers would arrive at the same conclusion in similar cases. In our morally pluralistic society it is impossible to appeal to universally accepted principles to settle the argument: a sufficient area of consensus to take care of the problematic cases does not exist. One is faced therefore not only with the intellectual problem of working out a moral and political philosophy adequate to deal with conflicts of responsibilities, but also with the task of justifying one's views to others who may hold to a different persuasion.

The second line of enquiry concerns how social workers manage conflicts of responsibility in practice. This is an empirical question on which little investigation has been done. The task of working out in principle how to deal with these conflicts is certainly daunting; but it would not seem that practical social workers actually spend much of their energy forever agonising over moral questions that have perplexed mankind since the beginning of civilisation. We suspect, therefore, that most social workers tacitly accept conventional standards much of the time, even where doing so contravenes their own beliefs; like any other social group, a profession exerts powerful pressures towards conformity. But we think it preferable for social workers to examine critically the conventional wisdom, to avoid the dangers of confusion, alienation, failed purpose, inauthenticity, and self-contradiction.

In the third sense we say that the worker is expected to act responsibly. This usually means respecting the relevant norms. An irresponsible action is one where the worker is considered to have departed from the norms of professional behaviour, for example by allowing someone to be exposed to undue risk, or where there is malevolent deception. Paradoxically therefore, the professional who claims the autonomy of responsible professional action with the implication that he himself will answer for the consequences, also accepts the constraint of acting within the relatively circumscribed limits of professionally responsible behaviour as defined by others, not himself. Professional autonomy is, at best, freedom to move within the boundaries of conduct legitimated by the profession. And here the paradox is doubled, for acting responsibly as professional norms dictate may even result in morally irresponsible action if the norms do not accord with the worker's own system of moral belief.

Responsibility in this third sense is, of course, closely related to the notion of self-determination. If we say that someone does, or should, act responsibly we must assume that he could potentially act otherwise: we reject determinism. Similarly, in adhering to a belief in promoting self-determination we naturally assume that a person is in fact capable of choosing different courses of action. Responsibility is impossible without self-determination; and trying to enhance someone's scope for self-determination implies a faith that he will, in the event, act responsibly.

From having responsibility, it is a short step conceptually and socially to having authority.[5] Professionals who say they undertake important responsibilities also demand the authority to discharge them, and of course they wish it to be accepted that it is their responsible exercise of authority which partly validates their claim to it. Authority is intrinsic to social work, but has a variety of contrasting aspects. Broadie (1978) identifies two major senses of the term, distinguished by the phrases it occupies. (i) A person may be *an* authority *on* a given topic. He has expert knowledge, and moreover is recognised as having it. Such a person is considered *authoritative* on his subject. Social workers claim expertise on a variety of topics, but in comparison with other professions the knowledge they claim to command is often felt to be debatable in its extent, dubious in its quality, or even non-existent. (ii) A person may be *in* authority *over* someone else. He has rights to expect the subordinate's conformity to his wishes in certain defined areas of behaviour, and again is recognised as having these rights. This kind of authority emerges most clearly in social work where the worker acts as agent of the legal system, as in probation.

The latter sense is closely related to a third sense also identified by Broadie. (iii) A person may act on someone else's authority: he has *authorisation* to do certain things, and may be said to act as that person's agent or representative. The same idea may equally be expressed as authority, or sanction, to do something; it may again be specified in terms of a set of rights. Now the worker may on occasion be authorised to act as the representative of society in general towards the client, corresponding to (ii) above; or by contrast, he may be acting as representative of his client towards others, including agencies of the state. For an example of the second case we could say that the client authorises the worker to pursue his, the client's, case for better treatment at the hands of the DHSS or the housing authority. It is very characteristic of social work that it must accommodate itself on both sides of this fence, sometimes even at the same time in the case of any particular client.

(iv) The fourth aspect of authority is primarily a matter of personal, psychological attributes than of knowledge or rights. A person may be said to possess authority in the sense that he will be skilful in gaining the compliance of others to his wishes. He will inspire admiration, respect, or fear. This quality of personal presence or charisma may well owe something to its possessor's knowledge and use of authority in senses (i) to (iii), and the conventional expectations engendered in others by their knowledge of this authority will perhaps tend to reinforce the possessor's psychological authority. We generally treat authority figures with deference, at least in the first instance. However, authority in senses (i) to (iii) and psychological authority are logically independent, and it is possible to possess one without the other.

A special kind of psychological authority is described by the term authoritarian:

An authoritarian authority must not merely have authority, he must exercise it in a way characterised by his tendency to over-ride or ignore the wishes, opinions, and feelings of his subordinates. (Broadie, 1978, p. 150)

Social work training places some weight on the student's grasp of, and relation to, authority. This may be thought of as comprising an understanding of authority in the various senses sketched here, an acceptance of their validity, and achieving adequate skills in the four areas. If a worker's practice is to be coherent he must achieve some kind of balance and integration between the elements of authority. A student who doubts the legitimacy of the authority in question may be said to have 'problems with authority', or if he lacks the conviction necessary to psychological authority he may be said to have difficulty in the 'use of authority'. Of course someone may have good arguments for rejecting the validity of a given authority. It is then most unreasonable to attribute the rejection made by him on rational grounds to some kind of psychological problem in him.

The concept of power is closely allied to authority and in some contexts the two terms are used almost interchangeably. We might say, for example, that the social worker has power to take a child into care, meaning little more than that he has authority in sense (ii) to do so. The traditional distinction has it that authority is founded upon moral or legal rights, or upon wisdom, whereas power denotes being in a position to coerce or constrain someone's actions without his knowledge or against his will. In reality authority and power tend to accompany each other. Power, however attained, will tend to acquire legitimacy with the passing of time, and thus take on the aspect of authority; those who usurp political power by non-constitutional means take care to fabricate a cloak of legitimate authority as soon as possible. Conversely, authority unsupported by power gradually evaporates leaving only the empty shell of formal authority. Given the volatile nature of power and authority and the variable usage of the terms, we do not think there is much point in trying to establish firm distinctions between them. The literature contains a fair number of descriptions of the ways in which social workers do, and should, exercise professional authority and power. The important point is, we suggest, to enquire about the basis of such statements, and specially whether they are descriptive or normative.

The last remark returns us to a constant theme of this chapter and the subject of the next. If professional authority is to be justified, it cannot be done merely by reference to a professional group's own internal construction of what constitutes valid knowledge for practice, but arguably must be subjected to the critical scrutiny of the community as a whole. Similarly it might be argued that the basis of professional power ought to be found in the context of the values of society in general, or else it must be counted as illegitimate. Authority evokes the corresponding idea of obligation, which is not only relevant within the confines of social work but also to the general problems of political organisation and responsibility.

Chapter three

Moral and political theory in social work

1 Introduction

In the first chapter we examined the concept of the person, the notion of respect for persons, and the implications of these ideas for social workers' treatment of persons. In Chapter 2 we saw that the rights of persons are qualified and relative. The focus of attention thus far has largely been, then, on what might be called short-range morality, concerned with face-to-face relations between individual persons and those others whom one's actions can be seen to affect directly. In the next section we outline alternative theoretical frameworks for the morality of interpersonal relationships. However, we must also take into account that social work is not carried out by practitioners acting alone in small, isolated and morally harmonious communities characterised by relatively simple forms of social organisation, but as part of the fabric of large and complex industrial societies and in consequence of political decisions. Social work necessarily has political as well as moral dimensions. We must therefore pay some attention to the general problem of how face-to-face morality can be integrated with, or at least reconciled to, the demands of political society, and in sections 3 and 4 we discuss political theory.

In this chapter we offer a very brief sketch of a few of the more pertinent concepts and problems from moral and political philosophy, and far more questions will be raised than answered. The reader must refer to the literature of those fields for fuller exposition and analysis.[1] We shall, however, propose that utility and justice each act as unifying threads which may be used to find one's way in what at first seems to be a field full of apparently unresolvable contradictions. In the final section we apply these ideas explicitly to social work.

2 Moral theories

Chapter 1 made some distinction between the concept of the person denoted in the principle of 'respecting the person' and the diverse range of attributes which 'persons' may acquire by a process of social ascription. In the abstract, the person is recognised for his essential worth as a human being; in actuality, persons live in socially, historically and culturally contingent worlds. To respect the person means something like acknowledging the moral status and significance of personhood. This implies that we may be required to show respect to total strangers: there are some persons whom we feel we ought to, or have a duty to, respect even outside the realms of our immediate family and friends. This is perhaps what is meant by those philosophers who speak about caring for the Other or the Stranger and in Christian terms perhaps recognising the demands of 'neighbour love', where the neighbour is anyone in need. Showing respect implies the recognition of the worth and dignity of all individuals irrespective of race, colour, creed or any other contingent attribute. There is, however, a fundamental question that has to be posed and though it may appear rather simple, the answer will inevitably involve an examination of basic ethical principles. The question is, quite simply, why? Why ought we to help others? Why ought we to care for others?

In his day-to-day work, the answer a social worker may give in justification of the adoption of a particular strategy with a client may, as we suggested earlier, be based on the skills and expertise acquired for the purpose of doing social work. However, his day-to-day work has of necessity to be based on more general principles about the moral values entailed in being a social worker. We shall see that philosophers have offered a number of frameworks from which the moral worth of any social and human activity can be appraised. We shall also see that though they often offer conflicting prescriptions they are not always mutually exclusive.

It could be argued that moral judgements and moral rules simply mirror convention – that what we ought to do in a particular situation can be determined by reference to what is actually done or what is generally believed ought to be done. However, it is widely acknowledged that an individual may wish not to comply with convention because he believes that conventional practices are morally wrong. It is on such an argument that rests the distinction between a 'positive' morality (the conventionally held beliefs about the morality or immorality of behaviour) and 'critical' morality (a personally developed moral framework in which the principles one adopts to guide his life and on which moral judgements are based).

47

The danger of accepting convention as the basis for making judgements about what ought to be done is that it comes close to saying that actions are right because they're right and leaves little scope for critical reflection on one's own moral outlook.

Philosophers have traditionally offered two types of theories in the search for a coherent basis for moral judgements: firstly, what are often referred to as consequentialist, utilitarian or teleological theories (for brevity, we shall refer to these collectively as consequentialist theories) and secondly, deontological theories.

(a) Consequentialist theories

For consequentialists, the moral worth of a single act or behaviour in general is to be assessed in terms of the good that results as a consequence. That is, moral worth is to be determined by the consequences of behaviour and not the behaviour itself. Actions are right or wrong insofar as they promote some form of good. Such a view is referred to as teleological in that the ultimate criterion of moral behaviour rests in the end (Greek *telos*) to be attained. The final appeal has to be to a good that is produced and it is on this perspective that rest consequentialist theories of moral obligation and moral value. Now there are, at the very least, two problems here which have been acknowledged by philosophers. These are (i) what good is to be sought: it is not immediately obvious that there will be total agreement about the nature of the good that is to be promoted; and (ii) whose good is to be promoted? Let us look at these in turn.

(i) The nature of good. What consequentialist theories have in common is, as we have seen, the commitment to the promotion of some good; where they differ is in what different philosophers have identified as being the good worthy of promotion. Amongst the ends deemed desirable have been included pleasure, happiness, power, knowledge, self-realisation and so on. Again what is interesting about such a list is that while it is the realisation of good which determines moral worth the actual 'goods' themselves have no moral status. That is, they are non-moral. For the consequentialist

> The moral quality or value of something is dependent on the comparative non-moral value of what they bring or try to bring about. For the moral quality or value of something to depend on the moral value of whatever it promotes would be circular. (Frankena, 1963, p. 13)

The logic of the consequentialist position is really quite straightforward. To know whether something ought to be done or whether it is right, the consequentialist is committed to the view that one must first know what is good (e.g. happiness, pleasure, etc.) and then work out whether the proposed action will produce the requisite good.

Perhaps the best known and one of the most important of the consequentialist theories is utilitarianism in which the moral worth of actions is determined by the greatest balance of good over evil. This was the position of Bentham and others for whom moral worth could be appraised in terms of the principle of utility or beneficence. Morally right behaviour is that which produces the greatest amount of happiness for the greatest number of people:

> Actions are right in proportion as they tend to promote
> happiness, wrong as they tend to promote the reverse of
> happiness. By happiness is intended pleasure and the absence
> of pain, by unhappiness pain and the privation of pleasure.
> (Mill, 1962a, p. 257)

The main point is that consequentialist theories look to the future in the judgement of moral worth. Hence utilitarian theories of punishment derive their justification from the consequences (reformation of the offender, deterrence of others, etc.) and not from the act of punishment in itself.

(ii) Whose good? One of the dangers of the utilitarian position is that, if the rightness or wrongness of actions are determined by the attainment of non-moral ends like happiness or pleasure, it is possible, on that basis, to justify using persons to attain specific ends in the interests of others. If the promotion of good is the greatest happiness of the greatest number of people, then there is little reason to respect the needs, wants, desires or claims of any individual in particular. On this argument it would, for example, be logically possible to justify the execution of an innocent man if it were thought that considerable benefit would accrue to society as a whole. Yet the traditional utilitarians did recognise this problem and in his essay, *On Liberty*, Mill (1962b) presented a theory of utilitarianism in which he sought to reconcile the claims of a consequentialist position with the liberty of individual men. Campbell (1975, p. 52) points out that Mill's utilitarianism is really a greatest benefit theory rather than a pure greatest happiness theory:

> To act rightly is to work towards the distributing as widely as
> possible of those human experiences (such as freedom, health,
> awareness of beauty and of truth), which bring the highest
> fulfilment to individual lives.

The argument in *On Liberty* is precisely to present a version of utilitarianism in which the individual does count and in which his interest or happiness is as important as the interest of others or of society as a whole. Nevertheless, a problem for the consequentialist position remains: the definition of what is good (which must surely be a matter of judgement) and the balancing of one person's good against that of others.

A further problem for utilitarianism turns on the distinction between rule- and act-utilitarianism. Should we be concerned to identify what action will produce the greatest good in each and every individual case or situation, as the foregoing discussion would seem to imply? Such a view is referred to as act-utilitarian. On this theory one would argue that although commonly held moral precepts may act as convenient guides or rules of thumb, nevertheless there is always the possibility that the greatest utility in specific situations may be served by disregarding the ordinary rules. The individual must therefore be prepared to consider every case on its merits. Against act-utilitarianism it may be objected that it is simply impracticable to calculate the consequences of every action, and so rules devised from an overall utilitarian framework must be devised. It may be thought that many individuals could not be relied upon to make the necessary calculation diligently and accurately, and that they require the guidance available from generations of moral teaching, which could be founded ultimately on utilitarian arguments. There is the possibility, depending on one's view of the good to be promoted, that the upholding of general moral precepts has itself a certain value in that it makes for stability and clarity of moral purpose. One might also devise a consequentialist morality which regarded, say, the principles of honesty and justice as themselves the goods to be promoted. But this would be stretching utilitarianism too far in that it would be difficult to reconcile with more straightforward versions based on happiness.

In answering the question of why we ought to care for or help others, it is also possible to argue that we should do so precisely because some good comes to the helper. This is recognised in the consequentialist theories of the *ethical egoists*. For the ethical egoists, a person's acts are right or wrong insofar as they promote a greater balance of good for himself. Now this may not appear to be a sufficient basis for morality and the main form of ethical egoism – psychological egoism – sounds more like a psychology of helping. This is because the only basis for acting morally is the amount of good or psychological wellbeing produced for the helper irrespective of the needs, wants or rights of others. That is, it is a theory of helping in which the rights of others to help or the obligation to help is derived from psychological and not moral considerations. This is not to say of course that egoistic impulses play no part in moral behaviour but rather that it does not appear to satisfy the ordinary notion of truly moral behaviour. It justifies the use of others as means in the pursuit of one's own ends and presents a rather one-sided view of morality which does not rest easily with the recognition of others as moral agents and as persons with their own claims.

(b) Deontological theories

Consequentialists argue that the moral worth of behaviour rests in its consequences. The deontological position is quite the opposite since the deontologists argue that the rightness or wrongness of behaviour has to reside in other than the promotion of some good. Actions can, they argue, be right even if the greatest good is not promoted and moral worth has somehow to be related to the act or behaviour itself. That is, acts can be seen to be morally right or wrong without reference to any consequent state of affairs.

The most consistently worked out deontological position is that of Immanuel Kant and we shall come to that presently. However, it is at this point worth noting a distinction between act-deontologists and rule-deontologists which parallels that between act- and rule-utilitarians. The distinction is important because of the difference in ethical standpoints proposed by philosophers in these two camps.

For the act-deontologist, only specific acts in specific situations can be judged in terms of rightness or wrongness. The act-deontologist, and here lies the important difference from the rule-deontologists, is committed to the view that there are no general principles or rules whether moral or otherwise that apply to all situations at all times. Since each state of affairs is unique the choices available to an individual are therefore also unique and the moral appropriateness of his action can only be judged in that context. The most well-known moral standpoint in this respect is *existentialism*. For the existentialists each state of affairs is unique and each person must decide in concrete terms what he must do and that choice is free from the restrictions imposed by any general standards or principles.

Rule-deontologists, on the other hand, argue that the rightness or wrongness of actions can be judged insofar as they reflect commitment to general principles. No action, argue the rule-deontologists, is altogether unique since it is always governed by some general standard or principle. Thus, the rule-deontologist would argue that we must always keep to our promises, we must always tell the truth, and so on. The difficulty with act-deontology is that the decision by X to perform a particular action in situation S imposes no obligation on X to do the same thing again in S, nor does it place any obligation on anyone else in situation S to do the same as X did. But if we are speaking about moral behaviour we are generally speaking about the duty or obligation we have to act in situations according to some general principles of morality. For the existentialist, he may feel he ought to act in a certain way but in no way accepts that it is his duty so to act nor that anyone else is morally obliged to act in that way. In short, we still have to find a basis for moral behaviour which explains why we ought to act in a certain way – or in other words what is morally right – and applies to other moral agents.

One of the problems with the deontological approach to moral behaviour, of doing one's duty or doing what is right, is that it often conflicts with our own interests and the interests of others. It may also conflict with our own happiness and the happiness of others. Thus there have to be clear criteria by which moral principles can be based on considerations of impartiality. It is in this respect that Kantian philosophy presents a framework for determining both how to decide what one's duty is and how to distinguish it from consideration of the consequences either for oneself or for others.

The obligation to act morally or do one's duty, suggests Kant, is like a command or conversely like a prohibition. Moral behaviour is governed by imperatives and Kant distinguishes between hypothetical imperatives which determine how we ought to act to attain certain ends (if you want to keep your friends, don't tell lies) and categorical imperatives. The idea of the categorical imperative is the bedrock of Kantian philosophy and he argues that there is one and only one categorical imperative which provides the basic principle for all moral behaviour. This is 'act only on that maxim which at the same time you can will to be a universal law' (quoted in Frankena, 1963, p. 25). It is this principle which allows the rational moral agent to ground his behaviour in a moral framework and it provides what Frankena asserts as a necessary and sufficient condition for determining what concrete maxims or rules we should live our lives by. It does so in at least three ways: (i) One can be said to be acting morally if one can will that the moral principle involved can be acted upon by everyone in similar circumstances. (This is the principle of universality which has been adopted by a number of philosophers as the determinant of morality.) (ii) Moral behaviour involves, therefore, acting through reason, and moral rules recognise the equal merit and worth of all persons who act through reason. (Moral principles are not self-evident, nor individually revealed, but are discovered through the exercise of reason.) (iii) Moral obligation and moral duty then are not situationally determined, nor is the behaviour of an individual to be seen in isolation, but in relation to a community of moral agents who in theory have equal status.

Now this is obviously a drastic simplification of a complex moral theory but it does serve to outline the basic differences between the consequentialist and deontological positions. And as we shall discuss further in this and the following chapters, there are good reasons for asking social workers to consider the possibilities of either tradition in providing some guidelines to the formulation of an individual moral standpoint. Both deontological and consequentialist theories offer valid frameworks which can be used to justify particular acts of social work or the practice of social work in general. In recognising the supreme worth of the self-determining rational being as an end, and never simply (though he may also be) a means to the ends of others, deontological theories contain elements that are plainly reflected in the principles to which social workers often subscribe. In particular, respect for the person is reminiscent of much from Kantian moral philosophy. On the other hand, despite the commitment to the individual, consequentialist philosophy has been an important factor in the evolution of welfare policy and the welfare state. Social work puts individuals into practical situations in which they deal with the lives of others and in which both deontological and consequentialist considerations may apparently have to be balanced. In particular, the commitment to the client as a person worthy of respect often seems to conflict with the needs of casework management, case allocation, the allocation of money, the determination of priorities, policy formulation and even work conditions.[2]

3 \ The relevance of political theory

What is the relevance of political theories to social work? It is fairly apparent that no account of the morality of interpersonal relations, however elaborate and subtle, can alone deal adequately with the considerations raised by the fact that people mostly live in societies very much larger than their own system of personal relationships. Societies have laws backed by coercive powers. They have governments which collect taxes, attempt to regulate economic activity, and send their citizens to fight in wars. In modern western societies almost no part of daily life is outside the reach of the state apparatus: nutrition, health, housing, education, industry, art, science, sport and much else besides are substantially controlled by the political organs. State-funded social work itself arguably represents an unwarranted intrusion into what have traditionally been seen as the most private and intimate areas of life, such as family relationships and personal life style. One might even wonder, in pessimistic mood, whether the influence of the state is not so pervasive as to make moral considerations impossible to apply and therefore irrelevant. For these reasons it is essential to consider the political as well as the moral dimensions within which social work is situated.

In discussing the import of political theory for social work we shall follow a somewhat similar strategy to that used in discussing moral theory. Beginning with a conception of the nature of persons, we discuss central political values, and thence political theories which attempt to give expression to these values. Certain political aspects of social work which were implicit but not fully developed in the discussion of rights and duties will be given further attention in the remaining chapters.

The starting point for any political philosophy concerns the nature of man, and his needs, which the polity must take account of. It poses similar empirical, epistemological and ontological questions as are faced by moral philosophers. In the discussion of the person in Chapter 1, we raised the problems of free-will and moral agency, and asserted their importance to the construction of systems of morality. It is, of course, quite possible to erect a political philosophy of a sort on premises that discount the reality of free-will, and to make prescriptions accordingly. Skinner's radical behaviourism is not merely a psychological theory – 'a self is a repertoire of behaviour appropriate to a given set of contingencies' (1972, p. 199) – but also implies a political philosophy if only in the negative sense that it denies the possibility that political philosophy can be meaningful. Hobbes's philosophy takes psychological egoism as axiomatic. However, the concept of the person which we have already put forward entails the major premises of rationality and the reality of moral agency, and given the centrality of those assumptions for social work one is committed to a political philosophy which makes similar assumptions. In other words the values generally associated with social work appear to be inconsistent with any concept of man that denies his capacity for moral agency, and this has implications for the kind of political philosophy that could be relevant in social work. Social work does not appear to be intelligible except in the context of the assumptions about man that have already been advanced. In addition to those notions of man as a moral agent, a polity must take into account the facts of men's needs. This presents different theoretical problems but is certainly not less important from the practical point of view. The political system must at minimum enable the provision of the means to a decent life, including food, shelter, education, and so forth, if it is to merit a serious call for our support, and a good deal of political philosophy is concerned precisely with how these needs can best be met. Many political idealists, aspiring to create a better world, would want to claim the relevance of other putative needs, such as those for peace, love, security, fulfilment, fellowship, learning, to a satisfactory political philosophy.

It is not difficult to see the relevance of these considerations to social work, which is commonly thought of as a way of responding to certain needs. It has sometimes been thought that the exact nature of human needs in general was in itself relatively unproblematical, and that the remaining problems of social living were essentially technical and would yield to the advance of better technologies for satisfying need. This somewhat complacent belief enjoyed a wide currency in the English-speaking world for some two decades after the Second World War. In Britain such a climate fostered the development of what we now call the welfare state. Similar assumptions on a grander scale underlay the 1969 Pearson Report on what was to be done about the problems of the 'developing' countries. Within social work there grew up a conception of human needs heavily influenced by the Freudian tradition, of which Towle's (1945) book on *Common Human Needs* is an interesting example. It is clear from the resurgence of interest in substantive political philosophy that this optimistic (or deluded) mood has now evaporated. Now social work, because of the task expected of it, faces in an acute and poignant way the fundamental problems of defining need. The belief that social work holds out the solution to meeting most of the, or even the most important, needs of those whom it serves is no more credible now than it ever has been. Social workers therefore require a political theory which offers an intelligible and coherent account of human needs in general, and those which social work has both the mandate and the capacity to respond to.

4 Political values

What are the basic values to which men desire their political systems to give concrete expression? Or, to put it another way, what are the goods which a political system should aim to safeguard and promote, and the evils to be minimised? Despite the great diversity of doctrines prevalent in contemporary societies, there is a surprising degree of unanimity on basic goals at least in the western tradition. Admittedly the agreement starts to break down pretty quickly once we ask exactly what each value stands for, and how the conflicting claims of each are to be reconciled. We shall take this up after first setting out the fundamental values.

(a) Justice and equality

Justice is not a unitary concept, but a complicated cluster of more or less connected ideas. It must be linked to equality because conceptions of social justice, as we shall see, must invoke some material principle of equality; a conception of social justice has to specify what it is that there should be equality of.[3]

The first distinction to be made is between justice in the narrow context of the legal system and justice in the broader sense of social justice. Legal justice is the object of legal systems: the purpose of the law is to uphold (legal) justice. On the other hand the object of social justice is the ideal society: Rawls (1972), p.3) says that 'justice is the first virtue of social institutions, as truth is of systems of thought.' The operation of the system of legal justice may contradict the requirements of social justice, and there are at least five ways in which the operation of a system of legal justice can be unjust.

(i) Mistakes. The legal system may deliver a result which is unjust by its own standards simply because one or more of the people involved in the case have made a mistake. This does not imply any intention to produce an unjust result, but the outcome can certainly be morally unfair or unjust. An example is mistaken identification by a witness, leading to a false conviction. Another example is mistaken understanding of the meaning of the law in question.

(ii) Perversion. The legal system may be deliberately manipulated to produce a result that is legally (necessarily) or morally (perhaps) unjust, as for example the 'planting' of evidence, 'fitting up', etc.

(iii) Failure of due process. If the proper procedures are not adhered to, the checks provided by the system may fail to operate, leading to unjust results. Alternatively justice may in fact be done, but it may not be seen to be done. Legal systems provide means (such as retrial and appeal) to cover such lapses, but for various reasons such as non-discovery, cost, etc. they cannot always be used.

(iv) Inaccessibility. If going to law is too costly, too difficult to understand, too threatening, or otherwise unavailable, the legal system cannot secure justice in that case.

(v) Unjust laws. This is in a different category from the other four in that the preceding items acknowledge the injustice of the result according to the system's own standards. This last case takes us on to the meaning of justice to be discussed below: the result is in keeping with the standards of the system of legal justice but is considered to be unjust by comparison with some non-legal, moral standard. For example, it may be quite justifiable in legal terms to implement laws which forbid private education, but it is arguable that such laws are morally unjust.

Moving on from legal justice, there are broadly speaking two contrasting concepts of social justice, or justice in the broadest sense. They sometimes give incompatible results.

(i) Justice as right. The idea here is that justice is brought about by ensuring that a person's rights are satisfied, and conversely that duties are done. This does not amount to more than a formal principle, for we still have to decide what the various rights and duties of members of society shall be. If a comprehensive theory of rights can be elaborated along the lines explored in Chapter 2, justice is then attained by seeing that they are fulfilled. In this context it is common to transpose the idea of rights into the language of desert – what one deserves by virtue of status, actions etc. The idea of rights or desert can be extended to include punishment for wrongdoing. We may either say that the offender deserves his punishment, or society as a whole has a right to punish him. This leads to the idea of retributive justice. However, the rights concept of justice soon encounters difficulties if left to do all the work of defining justice. It does not tell us how to resolve the issue if two or more persons have equivalent rights which cannot all be satisfied simultaneously. This problem frequently arises when distributing resources for social welfare. By what criteria, for example, should we decide which of two similarly needy and infirm old people ought to receive the single place in residential care that is available today? Also, it is far from easy to decide how classes of rights are to be earned. Some rights cost comparatively little, such as the right to free speech or the right to punishment, and can be distributed to everyone. But how shall we decide that A has a right to higher pay, or a better house, than B? Because of such difficulties much more interest is focused on a second approach.

(ii) Justice as fairness. The intuitive idea here is that everyone ought to be treated in the same way unless there are seen to be relevant differences. In the western tradition the ideal of equality of treatment has dominated thinking about social justice. In this context it is usually held that treating like cases alike and different cases differently is a purely formal principle of justice; it tells us the form of comparisons, but does not identify what are the relevant criteria of likeness and difference. The equality sought by theories of justice is not attainable merely by fulfilling the formal require- ment of treating like cases alike, but depends on a definition of what material principles apply. The adoption of equality as a first prin- ciple is not, we think, a logical prerequisite of a theory of justice; it is rather a value premise or a priori assumption. Fascism is one political philosophy which explicitly rejects equality. Nonetheless for most westerners there do not appear to be any serious conten- ders for the position of first principle having the powerful and widespread appeal of equality. Moreover the principle of equality is interdependent with the concept of the person; it is all persons who should be treated equally because the intrinsic nature of person-hood demands equality of treatment.

This concept of justice takes us then to the debate about distributive justice – what is it exactly that there should be equality of? Adapting the socialist maxim, we will review some of the principles that have been proposed for deciding what shall be given *to each*, and what shall be expected *from each*, member of society. There is no major problem about who shall receive what when the benefits in question are purely notional or non-material, such as the right to free speech; within the boundaries of full citizenship, all citizens have the same entitlement. Most modern political communities grant, at least in principle, certain fundamental human and political rights to all citizens. Certain categories of persons may not qualify for or may not have qualified for, or may be wholly or partly disqualified from, these rights; among them are slaves, children, criminals, the mentally incompetent, foreigners, etc. Whether or not the status of these excluded persons is just has to be decided by reference to a conception of rights, which takes us back to the first concept of justice discussed above. The problem of distributive justice focuses rather on goods which are limited by scarcity and which cannot be equally available to all. The most obvious of these is economic income, but we may broaden this to take in command over resources in the wider sense. In the social work context, the client's command over resources is affected among other things by the practical aids and services to which the social worker regulates access, such as money, home helps, and even skilled counselling.

The first approach to distributing command over resources is the simple one of perfect equality: everyone should receive the same monetary income or its equivalent. But the force of this somewhat drastic idea is much reduced by the thought that it is very hard to imagine an economic system that could possibly remain stable on the basis of equal shares for all, when experience tells us that substantial inequality seems inevitably to develop even where there exists a definite policy to the contrary. Some people will always be more equal than others. A second, even more serious objection is that equal shares for all would actually be unjust. This argument is based on the second approach to distributive justice, which is that command over resources should be distributed according to need. Equal need would attract equal resources. If A and B are both equally unhealthy, they should receive equal amounts of health care; but C, who is healthy, would receive very much less. This is a highly plausible and widely supported view, but also has to meet both logical and practical difficulties in putting it into effect. It is agreed I need food and shelter, but do I need a car or a television? How is one person's need for a heart transplant to be weighed against several thousand people's need for relief from rheumatism? Does one 'problem family' have more need for, say, one-eighth of a social worker's time than do several offenders waiting for court reports?

A third approach to distributing command over resources invokes merit in some form. Now merit is a broad concept, covering a range of attributes. It implies possession of certain excellencies of endowment or attainment. We may distinguish firstly between merit that is acquired without any intention on the part of its possessor, and that which does entail an intention. Merit without intention refers to natural endowment such as talents, beauty or intelligence, and perhaps certain character traits such as generosity. Merit of this sort appears to be removed from morality and might not seem a very promising basis for arriving at a just distribution of resources, but it is of course very important in reality; there can be no doubt that intelligence, for instance, does tend to earn its possessor a greater command over resources than might be the case in its absence. From a utilitarian point of view distributing command over resources according to non-intentional merit has quite a strong attraction, for it might well be held to promote the common good if the most talented members of society were to receive the greatest resources. Merit accompanied by intention can be classified into two sorts, moral and non-moral. Moral merit, which on the libertarian philosophy must of course be intentional if it is to count as moral, is the same as virtue. An approach to distributing command over resources based on virtue is deontological in character in that it tends to support actions which are defined as morally good in themselves. On the other hand merit which is intentional but non-moral refers to skills and abilities acquired by deliberately working for them but without any moral end necessarily in view, for example sporting prowess or musical virtuosity. Distributing command over resources by reference to non-moral merit is again utilitarian for it suggests that promotion of the general good should take precedence over rewarding moral virtue.

There are obviously major difficulties in basing a theory of distributive justice on a single one of the principles mentioned here, and many writers have suggested that several need to be combined. It is hard to deny the view that certain basic and fundamental needs should take precedence over less important ones; they should perhaps be satisfied on the principle of perfect equality. But defining basic needs is no simple matter. The idea of rewarding merit is problematic given that different people have different capacities for obtaining merit, whether moral or non-moral.

Turning now from the question of what each member of society should receive, let us briefly consider what they should be expected to give. One approach is to suggest that contribution to society should be based on a person's resources; such an idea seems to underlie progressive taxes on the relatively wealthy. Secondly we might propose contributions on the basis of abilities or endowments: the strong should perform manual labour, the artistically gifted become artists, etc. Thirdly we might suggest contribution on the basis of the rewards and privileges accorded to the person by society, such as education, inherited wealth, inherited status, etc. The idea of noblesse oblige comes into this category.

The modern debate on justice has been greatly influenced by the work of John Rawls, who has sought to find an alternative to utilitarianism on the one hand and intuitionism on the other. His theory relies on two basic principles of justice. It is thus much more economical than approaches relying on a multiplicity of principles, with their attendant problems of how to define categories such as 'basic needs', and possible conflicts between principles. Rawls's (1972) principles are (1) equality in the assignment of basic needs and resources and (2) social and economic inequalities are only just if they result in compensating benefits for everyone, and in particular for the least advantaged members of society. We cannot appraise Rawls's long and elaborated work here. Although much criticised, it continues to pose a formidable challenge, and has been well described (Ryan, 1981) as a theory which has survived any number of demolitions.

(b) Liberty

It would be safe to assume that everybody is in favour of freedom, while most people concede that it can never be absolute and some limitations have to be accepted as inevitable or desirable on balance. The ideal of liberty stands out as one of the pre-eminent political values right across the political spectrum and is the subject of a large philosophical literature. Here we introduce the topic by distinguishing four concepts of freedom and indicating the kind of specific content which each invokes.

(i) Freedom as the capacity for moral action. This is simply a restatement of the notion of free-will already discussed in Chapter 1. To hold that a person is free in this sense is to assert the libertarian thesis and reject determinism, or alternatively to adopt some form of compatibilism.

(ii) The major traditional concept of freedom is, perhaps, the idea that it means *freedom from* interference in one's life: in Berlin's (1969) terminology, it is negative freedom. To see what it means in practice we must ask at least three further questions: (1) in what respects is someone entitled to non-interference; (2) to what extent is this non-interference feasible; (3) is non-interference actually put into effect as a basis for political conduct? For example, we may say that freedom of speech and publication is an essential part of political liberty – it is one respect in which we wish to claim freedom from interference. We might then observe that even granting such a liberty in principle, there are inevitable practical constraints: not everyone is skilled in making their views known, or it may be impossible to get one's ideas printed and distributed at a price which people will be willing to pay. In connection with the third aspect we would want to question whether freedom of speech and publication was stifled by direct censorship, control of the means of dissemination, discrediting or defamatory propaganda, and so forth.

Negative freedom may be denoted, as above, by the phrase 'freedom of X' where X is a faculty or activity, such as assembly, religion, conscience. Freedom of X means the absence of intentional human interference in the pursuit of X. Alternatively we have the phrase 'freedom from Y', where Y is an agent or some product of human agency, such as means tests, conscription or arbitrary arrest. Freedom from Y means the absence of interference due to Y.

The content of negative freedoms leads directly to conceptions of rights. In saying that citizens have freedom of speech we imply that they have a right of free speech. The idea of rights is inextricably linked to the idea of freedom, and freedoms may well therefore be defined in terms of rights. This relationship was discussed in Chapter 2.

Although every political philosophy seems to espouse some sort of freedom, it is an overriding concern with negative freedom that has been the hallmark of the political tradition of liberalism. As such it is so much built into western culture that it may be quite difficult to stand back from that inheritance and evaluate it on its merits. Nevertheless the idea of negative freedom has not lacked its critics, as we shall now see.

(iii) The main rival to the ideal of negative freedom is of course positive freedom, which emphasises the necessity for *freedom to* do certain things or live a certain kind of life. It expresses dissatisfaction with negative freedom which may only mean freedom to starve; it asserts that mere non-interference does not guarantee that the individual shall have the material and moral necessities for a fulfilled life, which it is claimed is necessitated by the ideal of freedom properly understood. On this view therefore it may well be necessary to curtail the negative freedom of citizens in order to promote those goods which are essential to a fully human way of life. If, to take a familiar example, a person was never taught to read because compulsory schooling was regarded as an interference with his (negative) liberty, the price on the positive theory is a much greater loss of real freedom than the empty liberty of not going to school. Positive freedom therefore entails definite views on what is good for people. This is precisely what makes advocates of negative freedom suspicious – it seems to pave the way for meddlesome or even repressive policies.

It is arguable that the dominant conception of social work rests upon a concept of positive freedom. On this view social work is not merely a service to be provided in a neutral or passive manner for those who choose to make use of the kind of help it can offer. Rather, the proper function of social work is seen as actively promoting those resources and opportunities necessary for a decent life, and taking on wide welfare responsibilities even when the intended beneficiaries have not sought help. Such a position informs the Barclay Committee's (1982) advocacy of community social work, and this is simply the current expression of a social philosophy with a long lineage. Indeed it could be held that the mere fact that social work services are largely financed out of taxation means that they could not be justified on a negative concept of liberty, as they involve significant infringement of the taxpayer's freedom to spend his money. It will be seen that a positive concept of freedom greatly enlarges the area of justifiable paternalism. Mill's predominantly negative view of freedom caused him to take a vigorously anti-paternalist stance, whereby the harm a person might cause himself could never justify interfering with his freedom to do as he wished.

Conceptions of what is necessary for positive freedom are apt to be linked to conceptions of distributive justice. Whoever holds that certain opportunities ought to be provided will wish to ensure, as a matter of social justice, that they are provided to all those who should have access to them. Thus, for example, if we hold that it is necessary for the proper nurturing of human capacities that everyone should have access to the best medical care it is possible to provide, it is naturally seen as an injustice if some people are denied it through unsatisfactory social policies.

A certain conception of positive freedom underlies those social philosophies described as libertarian, whose aim is often denoted by the term liberation – in contrast to liberty.[4] They advocate freedom from repression, whether maintained physically by the state's instruments of power or morally by repressive norms, expectations and institutions. Some aspects of contemporary feminism, for example, reflect this orientation.

Liberalism and libertarianism are nowadays seen as competing philosophies. One represents the old right, the other the new left. Liberals are deeply mistrustful of the invasion of the rights of the individual that positive freedom seems to sanction; libertarians say that relying on negative freedom will never solve the real problems of the world. For all these differences it is perhaps worth remembering that a dream of freedom underlies both. Both are offspring of the move for human emancipation that characterises post-medieval western thought.

It is, moreover, a mistake to exaggerate the polarity between negative and positive freedom. Goodin (1982, p. 152) has argued that 'Positive and negative freedom . . . are not two different notions at all but only incomplete references to the same underlying conception of freedom.' This argument is based on MacCallum's (1967) formulation that freedom takes the form 'x is (is not) free from y to do (not do, become, know) z', where x ranges over agents, y ranges over such preventing conditions as constraints, restrictions, interferences, and barriers, and z ranges over actions or conditions of character or circumstance. Seen in this light, positive and negative freedom are not fundamentally irreconcilable concepts but rather reflect differences of emphasis or priority. Supporters of negative freedom believe that if we do not interfere with people's freedom, then fulfilment will take care of itself; supporters of positive freedom assume that it is not necessarily direct interference as such which is the main obstacle to a fully human life, but a lack of opportunities, due to unfavourable social conditions. Advocacy of either concept depends therefore not simply on one's moral values, but also on beliefs about how people and societies actually function. The concept of freedom one adopts necessarily entails psychological and sociological understanding as well as value judgements.

(iv) The fourth concept of freedom is paradoxical in that it proposes that freedom is attained by deliberately submerging the individual will in some higher entity. This idea appears in various forms in Christianity; in Rousseau's doctrine of the General Will; and in Hegel (Goodwin, 1982, p. 235; Benn and Peters, 1959, p. 213). Such a concept seems scarcely compatible with any robust notion of human agency. It is almost as if freedom consisted in not having to cope with the tiresome problem of deciding how to act. It contradicts the essentials of the concept of freedom of the individual and is somewhat out of sympathy with most of the western tradition. On the other hand a faint echo of it is found in some contemporary socialist views: 'The radical begins with a rejection of the liberal Kantian view of freedom, and sees both him or herself and fellow human beings achieving freedom in the context of the collective'. (Statham, 1978, p. 35). Radicals of course would hasten to say that they wished to assert freedom, not deny it. But freedom in the context of the collective must either mean some subjugation of the individual will, or imply a much weaker conception of the human capacity for moral action than the one we have adopted.

(c) Fellowship

In comparison with justice and liberty, the last three political values we shall mention are secondary. This is not so much because they are less highly valued as that they are generally understood as derivative from, or instrumental to, the first two. The ideal of fellowship expresses the hope that people will want and be able to live together in an atmosphere of positive regard for each other. They would share each other's pleasures and burdens; they would support each other and get to know each other well as whole persons. Similar ideals are alternatively expressed by the notions of fraternity and community. In essence the belief is that a fully human life is only possible in the context of multi-faceted, non-egocentric, non-exploitative relationships with one's fellow men. This may seem an unexceptionable aim, but it remains a matter of controversy how much people really care for each other's interests and how much they merely behave in a way which suggests altruistic motives because it serves their self-interest to do so. A wide spectrum of views has been expressed on this issue, from the most optimistic who hold that man's natural bent is benevolence to his fellow creatures, to the most pessimistic who hold that all men are intrinsically and essentially egoistic.

Social workers are sometimes expected to promote the good of fellowship; it is indeed built into the understanding of human needs that informs social work training and practice. Moreover community workers are sometimes thought to have the promotion of community spirit and identification as a major aim of their work, although this is probably much more often imputed to them by others than it is actually adopted by them. A positive valuation of community is also discernible in the idea of community social work, which we have already mentioned in the context of positive freedom. For all that, it is necessary to be very cautious about the misty romanticism often associated with the idea of community. Community has tended to degenerate into an almost meaningless epithet of approbation in discussion of social policy, as the following selection of terms indicates: community work, community care, community development, community action, community social work, community relations, community education, community policing, community councils, community newspapers, etc. Furthermore, popular uses of community are often based on sociological fiction, aggravated by the romanticism just referred to.

Before commenting on the remaining political values it needs to be noted that freedom, equality and community are by no means randomly chosen, unrelated goals of social life that might in principle be pursued independently of each other. Just as 'individual' and 'society' are concepts which can only be understood in relation to each other, so freedom and community are counterpart ideas. Freedom, in some sense, is essential to the possibility of community. We have already seen that freedom and equality are in some senses both opposed and complementary (a point elaborated by Charvet, 1981). The problems of how to reconcile and combine these various ideals, how to account for the social aspect of morality, and how to define the role of the state, have been and remain subjects of a great deal of philosophical speculation, particularly in the Continental tradition of Hegel and Rousseau.

(d) Happiness

Happiness is a self-evident political ideal in that everyone, presumably, is in favour of it. As it stands, however, it gives us virtually no specific guidance as to what the political community should aim to afford its members. In other words it is necessary to make clear what it is that happiness is supposed to consist of before one can aim to bring it about. Here again there is considerable controversy, dating back to classical times, as to the essentials of the good life. Without going into the various theories proposed we should note that views on this subject are very much a creature of culture and historical circumstance.[5] For example a popular debate is whether western countries' headlong pursuit of material consumption is necessary for, or antithetical to, the high ideal of happiness.

Happiness as a political ideal is bound up with the other ideals discussed in this section. Any specific conception of positive freedom must go hand in hand with a specific conception of happiness, because the positive freedoms deemed necessary or desirable would include freedoms to pursue happiness or fulfilment according to a given definition. The ideal of fellowship itself represents one such definition.

(e) Democracy

Democracy is nowadays very widely upheld and even taken for granted as a key political value, although as Plamenatz (1973, p. viii) points out, this was not always the case. It has, for example, been regarded as a pernicious and illusory doctrine liable to pave the way for mob rule according to the lowest instincts. Democratic is perhaps more often used as an evaluative term signifying approbation than as an analytic term describing a given sort of political system; it may be used just as a piece of rhetorical equipment.

We shall not analyse the various definitions of democracy or the merits of different models of democracy. Here we simply suggest that in contemporary terms it may most usefully be understood as an instrumental value whereby the other political values are promoted, notably justice and liberty. The good that democracy is intended to promote is derived from specific ideas of justice or freedom; it is unhelpful to see it as a good in itself.[6]

Strictly speaking, it is political systems which may be described as more or less democratic. However, democratic has acquired various secondary usages and is applied to such things as formal organisations (like social work area teams), and even individuals. Here it presumably denotes a high valuation upon consultation with others, shared or decentralised decision-making, and anti-elitism. It may imply openness with information, personal approachability and rejection of an attitude of personal superiority; it suggests that interpersonal relations should be of a footing of equal status, as opposed to deference. Democratic is used to mean the opposite of authoritarian. Although it may be somewhat inaccurate to talk of democracy in this extremely broad sense, the basic assumptions and values which motivate a concern for democratic ways are similar within the strictly political sphere and outside it. They include a conception of persons as moral agents possessing rationality, and a concern for a certain sort of equality as a prerequisite for justice.

5 Political theories

Political theories may be thought of as representing the attempt to reconcile political values of the sort discussed above with the problems of social living referred to at the outset of the previous section. They are concerned with the social arrangements necessary to harmonise, or at least make manageable, the competing interests of members of society. Political theories therefore analyse the nature of the state and the use of power. Goodwin (1982, p. 173) puts the problem thus: 'The fundamental task of political theory is to offer justifications for certain dispositions of power in a political system.'

Aside from physical force, the law is the main instrument whereby, under civilised conditions, the state exercises power and procures obedience to rules of conduct. Quinton (1967, p. 6) defines the relationship as follows:

A society is political, or has a state, if it contains a centralised agency for the promulgation, application and enforcement of rules of conduct, if these rules are generally obeyed and if only these rules are recognised as legitimately sanctioned by physical force.

The law defines the essential features of a political community. Many political theories seek to establish what framework of laws is logically justified given certain political values, and certain theories of social life. One outcome of such enquiries is to show that in the properly designed state there exists a general moral obligation to obey the law, as obeying the law is necessary to realise the political values identified.

It may be objected that the fact that people usually obey the law does not reflect any kind of moral obligation at all but is simply a matter either of prudence or expediency, or of coincidence. A full refutation of this point of view is only possible from the standpoint of specific social and political theories, but we can show initially that the prudence and coincidence arguments are, at least, implausible as complete accounts of lawful behaviour. The argument, firstly, that obeying the law is just a matter of prudence or expediency holds that we obey the law simply in order to avoid the unpleasant consequences, such as fines or imprisonment, that are liable to follow if we do not. This is a tolerable preliminary explanation of much law-abiding behaviour, especially perhaps in those areas where compliance or otherwise with the law is not seen to entail issues which are themselves of particular moral consequence. The shopkeeper who reluctantly observes the English legal restrictions on Sunday trading is probably right to reckon that defiance of the law would bring more trouble and expense than it was worth, but unless he is a Sabbatarian he may well regard opening his shop on Sunday rather than Monday in itself as morally indifferent. Furthermore, one's position at any time in respect of a particular law may be quite neutral in that one is not in a position either to comply or not comply with it. If I am not a shopkeeper I cannot meaningfully be said to observe or breach the laws on Sunday trading as they apply to shopkeepers.

The view that law observance is a matter of expediency seems to be reinforced by the commonplace observation that most people, for most of their time, follow personal habits and social custom. A certain value attaches to doing so which is independent of the merits of the action in their own right: conformity is psychologically more comfortable for most people than deviance. Now any law which opposes standard expectations and normal practices in the society to which it applies is likely to fall quickly into disrespect and disuse, unless it is enforced by drastic measures which have the effect of creating changes in standard practices. Much law-abiding behaviour is, then, essentially unthinking; one follows standard practices and incidentally complies with the law, rather than choosing deliberately to comply with it.

A second observation may be made to support the view that

obeying the law is not in itself an independent moral obligation, and this is that the requirements of morality and those of law are, as a matter of fact, generally in harmony with each other so that following a moral precept usually results in automatically abiding by the law, and vice versa. Provided that I refrain from murder, it might be said to be of no great importance whether I do so out of adherence to a moral principle or supposedly out of respect for the formal institution of the law. One might also claim that the law is, in general, a reflection or deduction from prevailing morals; that it is simply a formalised statement in a particular context of the generally accepted standards of moral behaviour.

Some theorists have regarded prudence as a sufficient, or nearly sufficient, explanation of lawful behaviour. On the other hand the main drift of political philosophy has rejected this explanation and considered that obeying the law is ultimately in itself a kind of moral obligation. After all it would seem on the face of it to be more than a mere coincidence that many legal requirements are often also requirements of morality, such as those prohibiting murder, exploitation, deceit, theft, etc. It is also not difficult to produce cases where compliance with the law seems to be against a straightforward notion of self-interest. We might instance the taxpayer who declares all his income even though the chances are that non-declaration will be more profitable. The view that law and morality are merely two manifestations of the same body of standards does not account for the constant independent changes in both law and morals. The admitted correspondence between large areas of the law and morality does not then provide any guide to action in those cases where law and morality are not in harmony, and these cases are in many ways the most theoretically interesting and the most problematic to resolve in real life. For instance, the legalisation of homosexual relations between consenting adults in private would appear to be regarded as a long overdue reform by some people but also as morally reprehensible by others. A somewhat similar difficulty arises when comparing standards in different countries: for example, polygamy is legal in some Islamic countries and illegal in western countries. If I emigrate to an Islamic country, it is far from obvious whether I thereby become morally entitled to practise the polygamy which is illegal in my western homeland. Even more awkward is the case of the man who legally practises polygamy in his country of origin and wishes to immigrate, with his wives, to a country which insists legally upon monogamy.

If we grant that the basis for the moral obligation to obey the law is a real and not a pseudo-problem, what do political theories have to say about it and about the proper role of the state in regulating social affairs? What kind of state is required? A large number of political theories have not only been proposed by academic philosophers but actually adopted as the basis of constitutional law and public policy within living memory. Most people would have no difficulty in recognising at least half a dozen, e.g. conservatism, fascism, socialism, communism, nationalism, totalitarianism. There are however various difficulties in approaching this area of theory and practice. Firstly there are no universally accepted consistent descriptive statements about the content of these theories. One man's democratic socialism is another man's totalitarian communism. Closely linked to this is the fact that labels for political philosophies are often used in a deliberately evaluative way, whether praising or pejoratively. Secondly the practical content of any given political philosophy is very much a matter of historical contingency. There was no need to worry about how or whether to conduct nuclear war until nuclear weapons were invented. Thirdly all practical political philosophies are arrived at by a process of historical evolution, with much borrowing from rivals' camps and adaptation to circumstances on the way; they are never put into practice in a pure form, despite the thought-experiments of philosophers. We cannot undertake a full presentation of these matters here; but to shed some light on the questions at issue, we shall adopt a fairly drastic simplification of political theory into two major traditions. These are liberalism and socialism. Our starting point is thus that much of the political theory which is still of interest and relevance can be understood as the competition between these two rival ideas of the ideal state and the individual's place in it.

Political philosophies must of course address the whole of social life, taking a broad view of what is relevant. Within any given sphere of activity there will be issues of special interest and concern that reflect broad political questions and orientations. In the field of social welfare, however, discussion of political-philosophical questions has been muted until recently. In Britain the postwar development of welfare services took place within a political culture that has largely taken its key objectives for granted. Latterly however there has been a marked resurgence of interest in the philosophy of welfare and the political assumptions implicit in state welfare services including social work. The academic discipline of social administration has been criticised for its lack of political analysis, and the contradictions implicit in the conventional approach to welfare have been under attack. As the conventional approach contains a blend of somewhat incompatible liberal and socialist assumptions it is not surprising that its weaknesses should have come to light, particularly given the ascendency of right-wing politics in Britain and elsewhere. From the other end of the spectrum Marxists have stopped looking upon the welfare state as a kind of minor epiphenomenon on the road to socialism, and started to develop Marxist analyses of this important area of social life. In this book we discuss the political basis of social work at various points; we must refer the reader to the literature on the philosophy of welfare to set social work in its wider context as one of the range of welfare services.[7]

(a) Liberalism

Liberalism is generally acknowledged to be the dominant political tradition of the western world. Despite this it is quite difficult to pin down what it means; the idea of liberalism is variable and elusive. This is well illustrated by the different connotations it carries in different contexts. In Britain liberalism is often regarded as vaguely centre-right, in contrast to the ideology of the labour movement or political libertarianism. The welfare professions are seen as a haven for 'woolly' liberals. The curious aspect of this characterisation is that these liberals are correctly seen as the heirs of nineteenth-century liberalism led by J.S. Mill, whose doctrines were regarded as radical for over a hundred years. In the United States however liberalism is associated with the political left, and is counterposed to conservatism – liberals are progressives, or were at least until recent times (Dworkin, 1978). In either country it is only from the context that one can judge whether calling someone a liberal is meant as a description, a compliment, or an insult. Despite being located at opposite ends of their respective political spectra, modern British and American liberalism seem to share a substantial body of belief.

In the course of the following discussion it will become apparent that a great part of what would nowadays be thought of, in ordinary political discourse, as conservatism is readily identifiable with some aspect or other of the liberal political tradition. On the whole conservatism is better understood as an inclination to preserve an idealisation of existing social arrangements, whatever they may be, than as a coherent doctrine in its own right. As liberalism has been the dominant tradition, conservatism has often worn the clothes of liberalism. (Older forms of conservatism exhibited an inclination to return to feudalism.) Contemporary radical conservatism has adopted a particular interpretation of liberalism that would in fact require substantial changes in existing social arrangements. Nonetheless we should not forget that liberalism is also associated with progressive movements.

The essential tenet of liberalism is the concept of negative freedom already discussed above. Much of its radical potential lies in its advocacy of non-interference in a range of activities that might be regarded as dangerous or immoral, especially in such areas as drug use or sexual behaviour. It is summed up by Mill's famous principle that the only ground for interfering with personal freedom is harm to others. For Mill liberty was essential to happiness and thus his whole utilitarian theory.

In section 4(a) above we proposed two contrasting concepts of social justice, one based on rights and the other on fairness. Liberalism associates easily with a concept of justice based on rights, as freedom from interference may naturally be posited as the basic human right from which other rights can be inferred. On the other hand utilitarianism by definition values greatest happiness above everything else, and its pursuit may well be thought to involve overturning a rights-based concept of justice in favour of a fairness concept. This contradiction, captured so clearly by Mill, has puzzled philosophers ever since. It also explains the progressive face of liberalism, with its support for the oppressed and its human sympathy.

Classical liberalism, concerned above all with negative freedom, associated readily too with laissez-faire capitalism; it is always suspicious of state intervention. Neoclassical liberals, notably Hayek and Nozick, have argued that this doctrine remains valid even in the context of late-twentieth-century capitalism. On the other hand the general drift of modern liberalism is definitely pro-interventionist in the economic arena, while arguing for non-interference in the area of personal morality.

Many theories of how the state should be organised have grown up in the liberal tradition, as a comparison of the constitutions of western countries quickly shows. It is characteristic of liberalism to insist on the essential nature of democracy, which has been seen as an indispensable attribute of the liberal state. However there are many different interpretations of democracy, none of them perhaps absolutely satisfactory from the theoretical point of view or entirely convincing on practical grounds.

Liberalism is predominantly individualistic in character. This means that in assessing social good the primary point of reference is taken to be the individual person and not some other entity such as the state or the community. Such political individualism may well be supported by a social theory which insists that the good of individual persons is the only meaningful good, as ultimately all social structures are reducible to individuals; on this view, it is simply nonsense to talk about social good as consisting of anything other than the good of individual persons.

The doctrine of respect for persons is frequently associated with or equated with liberalism. Goodwin (1982, p. 33) for example, identifies 'the preservation of the individual and the attainment of individual happiness' as the supreme goals of a liberal system. This is similar to the idea of negative freedom in that it invokes the notion of non-interference. Goodwin goes on to say 'This individualism is based on a morality which commends equal respect for all persons as moral beings with equal sensitivity.'

In similar vein both Statham (1978, p. 35) and a CCETSW (1976, pp. 22, 29) working party talk of the 'liberal Kantian view of freedom'. Nozick (1974) is a modern advocate of the idea that respect for persons necessarily leads to a classical liberal political system. Downie and Telfer (1980) give respect for persons the central place in their account of professional morality and analyse the politics of medicine and social work from an indubitably liberal standpoint. We think however that there is a danger of carrying the identification of political liberalism with respect for persons too far. Those who advocate a political system based on a premise of positive freedom do so precisely because they wish to cherish many of the same higher human attributes that respect for persons relies upon, such as rationality and the capacities for free choice and self-fulfilment. Social injustice affronts socialists because it makes impossible the realisation of the same human capacities and aspirations that the liberal wishes to preserve. Their quarrel with liberalism is not about the existence or value of these capacities, but on the correct means for enabling their expression. The humanistic side of the Marxist tradition, beginning with the young Marx and finding contemporary expression in such writers as Fromm and Marcuse positively rebels against the threat that men should not be masters of their own fate. In a recent article Keat (1982) has debated the relationship of liberal rights to Marxist social theory and sought to show that the latter does not deny, but rather assimilates, the former.

We do not think then that it can be justifiable to assume that respect for persons is intrinsically and necessarily bound to political liberalism; the relationship is more complicated than that. Political theories depend upon a specific conception of freedom, as we have seen. These in turn are only intelligible in terms of a specific conception of man. Any conception of man that rejects determinism tends very strongly to lead to a political theory in favour of freedom; the point at issue is not the necessity as such for freedom, but what exactly freedom should consist of. Although liberalism is conspicuous by its commitment to negative freedom, socialism has an inbuilt commitment to positive freedom which is nearly as strong. The precise content of the positive freedom sought is again dependent on one's views about man and the nature of social life; but as we have already remarked there is a similar dream of emancipation at the root of most modern western political thought.

(b) Socialism

In introducing the subject of liberalism we implied that it apparently referred to a wide range of political viewpoints and was difficult to define exactly. The same comment has to be made about socialism, and is inescapable given that we have adopted a simplification of political theory into just two broad tendencies. There are indeed many varieties of socialism, and as a matter of practical politics the attempt is often made to combine liberal and socialist prescriptions in the same political programme. This is particularly relevant for political parties of the centre, often identified as social-democratic, and centrist elements in otherwise liberal or socialist parties.

Despite these variations and overlaps the philosophical essentials of socialism are clear enough. Whereas liberalism is identified by its concern for negative freedom, the key element in socialism is a fairness concept of social justice. This means some form of egalitarianism, and inevitably economic inequalities are seen as the first that must be eliminated. Thus the burning issue for socialism is poverty. There are of course many views as to the material principles of equality that ought to be applied, and on the best means of reducing inequalities.

Socialism naturally adopts a positive concept of freedom; true freedom is seen as having the wherewithal to live a truly human life; the negation of this freedom is in itself an injustice. In particular this means that poverty is intolerable. In order to achieve the abolition of poverty it may very well be necessary to limit or remove certain negative freedoms. For example, the freedom to enjoy one's private property without interference cannot be allowed to stand in the way of redistributive measures which are necessary to abolish poverty. Nor is one person's ownership of substantial amounts of property likely to be compatible with the maximisation of the positive freedoms that others might enjoy if his property were redistributed.

Socialism is more concerned to procure the good of the entire community than to protect the arguably dubious interests of those individuals whose privileged position might make them vulnerable if certain freedoms from interference were not protected. Socialism embraces a conception of social life which emphasises the collective aspect – at the expense, liberals would say, of the individual. The ideal of fraternity is a natural corollary of the abolition of social injustice and the promotion of the wider social good. In the ideology of cooperation, socialist economic structures link together the technical means for combating poverty with social institutions intended to promote egalitarian and mutually interdependent social relations. This contrasts markedly with the individualism of capitalist social relations.

Because socialism aims for the implementation of an egalitarian conception of social justice it is much more likely to countenance the active intervention of the state in all spheres of social life than is liberalism. Positive steps are necessary to reduce inequalities and pursue social objectives. Many, though not all, versions of socialism require a comprehensive state apparatus, and it is arguable that historically no enduring form of socialism has been achieved in modern times without a powerful state. For many socialists the state ought in principle to be a benign agency whose existence is essential to the pursuit of many vital social purposes; this contrasts with liberalism which tends to the view that the state should have only those functions minimally necessary to protect basic negative freedoms. Socialism sees the state as a necessary instrument of beneficial social change and is therefore much less preoccupied with the problem of political obligation which vexes liberals. On the other hand traditional Marxism regards the very existence of the state as merely an evolutionary stage in the process of the development of true socialism. Modern Marxism has become concerned with the way a powerfully interventionist state has in western societies apparently come to serve the anti-socialist interests of capitalism.

Mention of Marxism brings us to the predominant socialist theory; virtually all modern forms of socialism have a large debt to Marx even though they may not wish to be thought of as Marxist. However, Marxism represents not merely the views of a single nineteenth-century political economist but a diverse and extremely vigorous tradition of philosophical and social thought. Amongst the central topics of Marxism are the following: a theory of knowledge – the dialectic; social theory – materialism, historical determinism, class, production and reproduction; economic theory – capital, surplus value; political theory – how to bring about change, and the goals of social life. The power of Marxism lies precisely in its breadth of coverage of these diverse but fundamentally interrelated subjects, and the way in which insights from one area of enquiry are brought to bear with telling effect in another. It is beyond our scope to attempt an account of this field here, and probably superfluous as there are of course numerous explications available of Marx's theories and of Marxism. In the context of our discussion of socialism as the major alternative political philosophy to liberalism the point to be made is this. Marxism offers a compelling theoretical analysis of the economic and other inequalities which offend the socialist's conception of social justice. It shows how these inequalities are not merely unfortunate and remediable side effects of classical liberal economic models, but essential to their very structure. Class structure and class consciousness are seen as fundamental obstacles to a socialist society. The abolition of privately

claims to show

held capital is necessary to achieve the political and humanitarian goals of socialism. Marxism thus proposes many of the features that a socialist society should aim to incorporate, and the practical methods which should be followed to bring about the change. What also needs to be said is that Marxism itself is an extremely diverse tradition which frequently generates theoretical inconsistencies and opposing prescriptions for action.

Marxism has never been the official philosophy of any of the western so-called liberal democracies which represent the homeland of social work – indeed the classification of a country as a liberal democracy is virtually contingent upon its being avowedly non-Marxist. Despite this, Marxism is enormously influential and now overshadows all other conceptions of socialism. The programmes of socialist parties throughout the western world incorporate greater or lesser borrowings from Marxism. Contemporary Marxism in its turn has energetically pursued the task of adapting and developing the essential principles of Marx's theories to the many aspects of the modern world he did not anticipate.

6 Social work, utility and justice

In this final section we shall review some of the foregoing conclusions and comment on the relevance to social work of the issues raised. We will aim to show that although there are no simple or straightforward solutions to the problems of establishing the boundaries of moral and political obligation, nevertheless it is possible to establish some landmarks which render more intelligible the moral and political judgements which social workers must inevitably make. In particular we shall argue that the boundaries of moral action can be related to the specific conception one attaches to the central ideas of utility and justice.

In section 2 of this chapter we surveyed theories of morality and drew attention in particular to the tension between consequentialism, and particularly utilitarianism, and deontology. Social work embodies much from both families of theories, and we deal first with utilitarianism. As a practical philosophy of reform utilitarianism played a key role in the series of social and legal developments which led from the Poor Law of the early nineteenth century to the welfare state of the mid-twentieth, and social work as it is now understood is very much a product of these developments. Utilitarian ways of thinking are so engrained into the fabric of contemporary social services that it is quite easy to forget their presence. A couple of examples may act as reminders.[8]

The Seebohm Report (1968) called for the reorganisation of the personal social services on the following grounds, inter alia: to attract more resources; to meet needs on the basis of overall requirements of the individual or family; to meet needs at present neglected. The conception of need implicit here is utilitarian; having a need implies lacking a good whose possession is, in an important way, conducive to happiness. In this view social work should attempt to maximise the welfare of its clients and that of the community as a whole. Such a position may seem uncontroversial or even obvious. But it would not be outside the broad tradition of social work to suggest, on the contrary, that the proper responsibility of social work is to promote certain ways of living: some such assumption seems indispensable to the probation officer, for example. It is interesting to speculate what the Seebohm Report might have said if it had assumed that correcting the ways of the morally weak or defective was one of the main aims of the social services.

In his recent introductory textbook Martin Davies (1981, pp. 137–8) proposed that the role of social work in society should be understood as maintenance: 'Social workers are the maintenance mechanics oiling the interpersonal wheels of the community . . . [their] acts are intended to contribute to a smoother running society.' The utilitarianism of this notion of social work is again fairly evident. The social worker (or social engineer) fixes things when that smooth running is disrupted by personal or systemic inadequacies. What this conception does not properly allow for is the possibility that the smooth-running society may be unjust; one can for example have a smooth-running dictatorship.

The point we are making, then, is that the development of social work and social welfare generally have been profoundly influenced by the utilitarian philosophy. Wilkes (1981, p. 63) comes to a similar conclusion: 'consciously or unconsciously, social work thinking is, for the most part, sympathetic with utilitarian modes of thought in that the worth of a policy or action is measured against its tendency to produce "good" results.'

Any plausible statement of the purposes of social work will include reference to the promotion of some good such as alleviation of distress, self-realisation, promoting welfare, or the like, and with it the explicit or covert expectation that what promotes most good is better social work. But this does not amount to a claim that most, or even many, social workers are utilitarians; that is still an open question and, given the difficulty of classifying most people's only fairly approximate moral views, could well remain so. Rather, the enterprise of social work has much in common with the other social reforms of the last 150 years in that the benefits to society as a whole were expected to outweigh the disadvantages to some of those directly affected, and the taxpayer who had to pay for them. Social work can certainly be understood as part of society's defence against the embarrassment of poverty, the threat to order posed by lawbreaking, insanity, and other forms of deviance, and the moral fright induced by the wicked. On the other hand it is perfectly plausible to suppose that many social workers do, in fact, incorporate a utilitarian element into their personal morality. Utilitarianism is philosophically powerful, and has dominated the culture of the historical period which has engendered social work. It is only to be expected that social workers have, as others have, absorbed to a certain extent the ideas of utilitarianism and made them part of their ordinary moral consciousness.

To discover the deontological element in social work we need look no further than any standard discussion of social work values, where the concept of respect for persons, and its analogues and derivatives, figure so largely. It is, admittedly, a matter of debate whether respect for persons is to be understood on the one hand as a moral given or absolute, requiring and allowing of no further justification, or on the other as a concept deducible from more basic premises such as human rationality or the existence of God. Plant (1970, p. 13), who provides a valuable analysis of this and related questions, suggests that respect for persons 'is in casework literature, more often presupposed than argued for' and goes on to argue that respect for persons is 'not itself a moral principle, but is rather a presupposition of morality'. Downie and Telfer (1969) take a similar view. But it is not necessary to finalise one's position on the justification of respect for persons to recognise its deontological character. In asserting the value of each individual person, it clearly contrasts with the utilitarian aim of promoting the common good. Utilitarian arguments may be extended to all sentient creatures, and lead to arguments for drastic revision of our treatment of animals; in some circumstances they would deserve better treatment than some humans. Such a view is in complete contrast to treating persons as ends not comparable to any other entity. Vlastos (1969, p. 148) states the deontological position thus: 'everything other than a person can only have value for a person'. In noting this element in social work we are not saying that all social workers are deontologists, any more than we were saying earlier that they are all utilitarians. But if respect for persons is more than an empty professional formula, it seems to commit social work to a deontological morality.

Moving now to political theories, in section 4 of this chapter we made a comparison of liberalism and socialism, and portrayed the arena of political theory as expressing a perpetual tension between the two. Again we see that social work incorporates much from both traditions. The liberalism in social work is not at all difficult to discern. Both liberalism and social work have a strong tendency to individualism. Liberalism is committed to protect the rights and freedoms of the individual. Social work has in general been over-whelmingly concerned both in theory and practice with the service given by the worker to the individual client. Although there have always been elements wishing to stress the reformist nature and broad social purpose of social work, the fact is that social work with individuals on a one-to-one basis has long been seen as the heart-land of social work. Indeed there is a not insubstantial body of opinion which considers broadly collectivist concerns with the social fabric as a whole to be outside the realms of social work. Social work has rarely been noticeably effective in securing the kind of political changes that a collectivist perspective would require, and does not direct most of its energies in that direction.

The traditional conception of the professional role in social work has a markedly liberal character. Butrym (1976) gives a defence of professionalism which relies on four elements: (1) service orienta-tion – not putting worker's interests before client's, (2) social usefulness of social work, (3) enhanced effectiveness, (4) responsi-bilities held by professionals in trust for society. Now this concep-tion of the place of a profession places a very definite distance between the organs of the state and the professionals. The profes-sional is supposed to operate with substantial independence and with no direct political control; there is only a broad social mandate. This stems from the same concern for negative freedom that informs liberalism: the rights of both worker and client need to be protected from interference. Further, the idea that social workers are guardians of a social trust is very reminiscent of the idea of social contract in liberal political theory. It also recalls the liberal doctrine of separation of powers.

Social work is often represented as a kind of creative compromise between care and compassion for the weak, and control of the deviant. From a liberal point of view a compromise is needed to reconcile the anti-humanitarian consequences of unmet needs with the general presumption in favour of negative liberty. But from a Marxist point of view the problem of unmet need cannot be fully analysed except in terms of the conflict of class interests. In addition the functionalist sociology which informs Butrym's defence of professionalisation provides a natural partner to political liberal-ism, but is quite unacceptable from a Marxist point of view.

Although social work derives many of its basic assumptions from the predominantly liberal political culture which has engendered it, nevertheless socialism too has made a significant contribution. The fact that social workers and socialists are sometimes confused in the popular imagination is not simply an etymological accident. The policies that tend to promote increased spending on welfare services including social work are nearly always the product of left-of-centre governments, whereas right-of-centre governments notoriously begrudge welfare spending. Then there is the very important fact that in many situations social workers typically devote their resources to the poor and deprived sections of the population who would presumably have most to gain under the kind of redistributive policies favoured by socialism. Many people would hold that this is precisely where social work ought to be concentrated. Thus both social work and socialism seem to have the benefit of the poor as a central object. This is not to forget that much social work has little or nothing to do with poverty, nor that socialism aims for the benefit of the whole of society and not just the poor. Earlier we commented that a positive concept of freedom seems to dominate in social work, which indicates a sympathy with socialism. Finally, although there seems to be little systematic evidence on the subject, it is safe to assume that many social workers are socialist in their general political persuasion, and that it is this same impulse which informs their commitment to social work. In Chapter 5 we shall have more to say about radical social work.

Utility and justice

The aim of this chapter has been to give a simplified account of the major questions of moral and political philosophy in terms of a relatively small number of key issues, and illustrate their application to social work. While it is not our intention to advance or defend any specific moral or political theory, it may be rather disorienting to leave the subject without having come to any definite conclusions. In this final comment we propose that the two principles of utility and justice may be used to arrive at a definition of the specific ends of moral and political theory. Our approach thus follows that of a good many contemporary philosophers who have come to the conclusion that a monistic moral or political theory, built on a single principle, cannot succeed. Utility and justice can be regarded as intermediate variables between basic values on the one hand and substantive moral and political theory on the other. They must be thought of not as unitary moral values but as constellations of values.

Utility, or the promotion of the common good, must be the object of any plausible theory of obligation. This much is uncontroversial, but its interpretation is a matter of debate; utility is an 'essentially contested concept'[9] whose meaning is necessarily variable. We have seen that utility is the key to the most important consequentialist theories, which assess the moral worth of actions according to the amount of non-moral good they procure. There are however many different versions of utilitarianism: the non-moral good we wish to procure may be pleasure, happiness, benefit, etc. If it is accepted that freedom, like happiness, can be treated as a non-moral good – that is, that being free is not in itself a *morally* good or bad thing – then the utilitarian framework can be adapted to the political dimension. If we define the good of man as negative freedom, the notion of utility leads directly to political liberalism. Alternatively a definition in terms of positive freedom leads to socialism.

Justice is also an essentially contested concept. In the sphere of personal morality a certain version of justice can be identified with deontology. Deontology claims that actions are intrinsically morally right or wrong; and justice may be seen as a matter of satisfying moral rights which follow directly from the same premises that determine what are morally correct actions. Thus respect for persons is the key principle of morality, and justice consists in according people the rights that follow from respecting them as persons. Conversely negating these rights is an injustice. Rawls (1972, p. 30) takes the view that justice is by definition a deontological concept in that it is non-utilitarian. A natural extension of the scope of individual rights leads us into the political sphere and here an idea of justice provides a foundation for political liberalism.

A markedly different version of justice inspires alternative political theories, as we have seen. Where justice is interpreted as some form of egalitarianism – the need for equal treatment in certain defined respects – a variety of socialism is the more likely outcome. However a number of liberal theorists have argued for forms of egalitarianism which would not be seen as adequate to procure justice by most socialists.

It will be seen that adopting utility and justice as the intermediate variables in moral and political theory does not of itself solve any substantive problems. The point of the approach we are suggesting is that it offers a way of tackling the central questions. If we can decide exactly what conceptions of utility and justice we favour we can move towards theories which address the substantive problems. It would also seem that neither utility nor justice can be excluded from a comprehensive moral and political theory, or one reduced to the other (although utilitarians generally hold that the principles of justice are contained within utility – looking after utility takes care of justice automatically). We are left then with utility and justice as two separate though not necessarily conflicting principles of morals and politics. This is similar to what Frankena (1963) terms a 'mixed deontological' approach, which is not unrepresentative of contemporary thinking. It makes more intelligible the mixture of moral and political principles which people seem to hold, and which we have polarised for the sake of argument. This approach of course does

not do away with basic conflicts of value; but that eventuality is
unlikely ever to arise.

Chapter four

Professional ethics and politics

1 Whose responsibility?

In the summer of 1981 an extended pay dispute between the
government and the civil service unions, whose members staff the
income maintenance service, resulted in disruption to social security payments. The result was that many claimants were left with no
money for daily needs, and there were quite a few cases of real
hardship. Some of these unfortunate claimants turned, naturally
enough, to the social work department for help. In Scotland's
Lothian Region they were disappointed: notices were prominently
placed in the reception areas of local offices to the effect that the
social work department would not entertain requests for financial
assistance in such cases.

There is a host of potentially good arguments – pragmatic, ethical
and political – for such a course of action. Some of them might go
like this. (i) 'It's not our job.' Social work agencies do not, in
Britain, exist to meet basic subsistence requirements. As social
workers, we would therefore be exceeding the duties imposed by
society through legislation. Besides, we are not technically or
practically equipped to deal with financial support to clients in a fair
or consistent way. (ii) 'We can't afford it.' Social work resources are
limited: they ought to be applied strictly to the purposes for which
they were raised. To do otherwise would be a misappropriation of
public funds. In any case social work could not bear the large
financial burden of income maintenance services. (iii) 'It would
weaken the civil servants' position.' The civil servants, themselves
lowly paid, have justice on their side in their fight with the government over pay. We should not relieve the government of its
embarrassment at afflicting the poorest in society. The unity of the
labour movement requires solidarity with the civil servants.

Clearly views such as these have a certain force, and could be used to fend off unwelcome demands arising from circumstances beyond the control of social workers and their clients. But a moment's comparison with the arguments of our earlier chapters reveals an uncomfortable inconsistency. Respect for persons would seem to entail some sort of obligation to do whatever one reasonably could to assist someone deprived of the means of subsistence to obtain them. Clients presumably have at least a qualified right to expect their social workers to do something practical about immediate, pressing and basic needs. On the face of it the frustrated claimants would seem to have a first-rate call on the considerable resources of social work. The technical difficulties were not, after all, insuperable: faced with the same situation, nearby Strathclyde Region set up temporary arrangements to fill the financial gap and recoup the funds later from the DHSS.

The first argument of this chapter will be that a social worker's professional ethics and the political issues surrounding social work practice cannot be understood or treated in isolation from each other. Social work has prided itself on its dual commitment to 'individual' and 'society', to inner and outer realities, but has been slow in practice if not in theory to grasp that one cannot intelligibly be grasped without the other. It is as short-sighted for a social worker to regard himself as 'non-political', interested only in the welfare of his clients as individual persons, as it is for a community activist to claim an interest in political issues to the exclusion of the predicament of the individuals he actually works with. Equally, it is a misconception to treat professional ethics as a gloss on the main body of social work practice, or as an area of rarefied speculation that need seldom bother the practical social worker. It will further be argued that ethical principles and practice precepts must also be considered in their mutual relationship.

2 Professional ethics

The term 'ethics' is used with several shades of meaning which need to be distinguished for the purposes of this discussion.[1] In the first place it may simply refer to a branch of philosophy, and is roughly synonymous with 'moral philosophy'; ethics in this sense is concerned with the premises, analysis and argument surrounding conceptions of right conduct and the good life. This book draws heavily on ethics as an academic discipline.

In the particular context of professional conduct 'ethics' acquires a different aspect; it refers to certain rules and procedures devised for the regulation of professional conduct. An action is ethical or unethical according to whether it conforms to these rules, or 'codes of ethics'. Moral philosophy and professional ethics have, to be sure, certain concerns in common; but precepts for professionally ethical behaviour may come to seem very remote from ordinary notions of moral behaviour. For example, in medicine the term 'ethical' is applied to drugs available only on prescription; the International Code of Nursing Ethics includes the statement that 'the nurse is entitled to just remuneration' (quoted in Campbell, 1975); the code of the British Association of Social Workers includes the statement that 'continuing professional education and training are basic to the practice of social work' (BASW, 1977); and many professional codes prohibit individual practitioners from advertising.

A code of professional ethics seems to be regarded as an essential accomplishment of a properly established service profession. The National Association of Social Workers adopted its formal code of ethics in 1960, and the British Association of Social Workers its code in 1976. It is not insignificant that a formalised code of ethics appeared necessary so long after the emergence of social work as a distinctive activity. Butrym (1976, p. 56) comments: 'The slowness on the part of British social workers to formulate a code of professional ethics is striking when viewed from the perspective of social work as a predominantly moral activity.' If the generations of American and British social workers who practised before these dates managed well enough without a formalised code of ethics, it is at least questionable that a formal statement adds anything to their inheritors' understanding. Whatever the improvements in knowledge that may have been attained by later generations, it is not suggested that the first social workers were less ethical than modern ones. The specific ends of their professional activity may have been different: for example, poverty may once have been regarded as a reflection of personal inadequacy. But one may assume that they pursued their aims with the same degree of good faith as contemporary social workers. The emergence of codes of professional ethics in social work is probably better accounted for by increased aspirations to the full status of personal service profession than by an increased concern with high principle. Many of social work's first principles or ground rules have been borrowed from medicine: the notions of aetiological explanation, diagnosis, treatment, and the professional's mastery of a body of scientifically valid specialised knowledge indicate analogies whose origins social workers have almost forgotten. So it is perhaps not surprising that social workers should follow medicine in believing in the desirability of a code of ethics. The application of the idea, however, is not at all simple.

An inspection of nurses' and social workers' ethical codes reveals an ambiguity as to the kind of statements that comprise such a code. One might expect a code of ethics to contain largely normative statements of the type: the professional ought/ought not to do . . . . A similar idea may alternatively be expressed in the form of a pledge: I will/will not do . . . . The Geneva Convention Code of Medical Ethics contains, for example, the statement 'I will maintain utmost respect for human life' (quoted in Campbell, 1975). The NASW code contains the pledge: 'I regard as my primary obligation the welfare of the individual or group served, which includes action for improving social conditions' (Morris et al., 1971). Besides these prescriptive statements, the codes of social workers and nurses contain much that is apparently framed in descriptive terms. From the BASW code come statements of the form: 'social work has developed methods of practice, which rely on a growing body of systematic knowledge and experience.' A similarly descriptive class of statement appears in the International Code of Nursing Ethics: 'nurses . . . stress the prevention of illness and promotion of health by teaching and example.' It is unclear in what sense these can be ethical statements, unless they are intended to denote professional aspirations in spite of their indicative form. The principles purportedly underlying the codes are not translated into any clear or complete statement of rights and duties; indeed the social work codes seem to have much more to say about professionals' rights than clients'.

Social workers' ethical codes seem, then, to suffer from a deep-seated ambiguity, or perhaps lack of clarity, as to what kind of statement they are trying to make. They also suffer from difficulties of application which are ultimately crippling. Let us return for a moment to the problem in Lothian Region and imagine a thoughtful social worker's perplexity when confronted by a destitute client needing money. The BASW code asserts in uncompromising terms the principle of respect for persons and the duty to prevent hardship; clearly the client's needs are not lightly to be brushed aside. Moreover the BASW code proclaims that social work has a duty to 'bring to the attention of those in power, and of the general public, ways in which the activities of government, society or agencies, create or contribute to hardship or suffering or militate against their relief.' On the other hand social workers are acknowledged to be accountable to those under whose authority they work. The worker is thus faced with a dilemma, but the code of ethics does not help him resolve it.

It may be replied that the purpose of a code of ethics is not to provide comprehensive guidance for every conceivable situation, but to lay down broad principles. Nothing is to be gained by insistence on casuistic application of this or that clause; rather, the worker must make up his own mind on the basis of general principles. Any moral system is apt to generate dilemmas, and if this is also true of professional codes of ethics, that is no condemnation of them. The codes themselves state that broad principles are intended, not minute guidance.

This defence is of limited value. It is unreasonable to suppose that social work's ethical principles, like those of other professions, would be anything other than broadly in accord with the moral norms of the society which sustains the enterprise. In the case of social work, there can be little doubt that its broad principles or values are directly descended from the western and specifically Christian tradition. The BASW code can substantially be reduced to the following principles, stated in shorthand terms: (i) respect for persons, (ii) special rights and duties by virtue of professional role, (iii) importance of knowledge and skill for performance of role. The codes then do not add much of consequence to the social worker's own moral understanding gained from his ordinary life experience. They fail to provide guidance precisely at the point where dilemmas specific to the practice of social work arise. It is not surprising that they seem to be treated with indifference by most social workers. Pearson (1975b, p. 55) puts it trenchantly: 'essentially, social work's value system, as a scheme for action, is *empty*.' He specifies three respects in which traditional views of social work ethics are inadequate: (i) the principle of individuation is not operationalised, (ii) clients' rights are stated, but not the limits of them, and the code of rights is inadequate to meet practical concerns, (iii) values are reconceptualised as techniques.

The disembodied notion of professional ethics, as articulated by the professional organisations, must be rejected as an inadequate conception of the problem. Abstracted ethical principles lose their point when divorced from the totality of practice situations. Practical guidance for the worker faced with the Lothian Region problem would have to comprehend the personal, ethical, organisational, political and practical aspects. Ethical principles for practice cannot stand apart from what Siporin (1975) terms 'technical' practice principles; rather, the problem is to assess the ethicality of practice principles, that is, the extent to which practice principles embody ethical precepts.

An important corollary of this argument is that social work is *intrinsically* a moral endeavour. It is not just a set of more or less value-neutral technical skills, able to be applied to a variety of moral ends; rather, any approach to social work must necessarily entail a moral significance. Emmet (1967, pp. 15–16) stated the point succinctly:

In a profession such as medicine, the professional code is designed so that the doctor can properly carry out a generally accepted and recognised purpose. His professional ethics are primarily concerned with means. But in the case of some professions, notably social work and education, the end itself is controversial and difficult to state, and any way of stating it is likely to have some ethical notion built into it, either overtly or in a concealed way.

The fact that social work must entail a moral purpose points to the relevance of the moral theories discussed in the previous chapter. But although the main stream of social work, at any rate, is defined by its commitment to respect for persons, self-determination and so on, the professional codes of ethics have only a vague and distant relationship with any clearly discernible moral doctrine. As we have already argued, concepts such as respect for persons will only serve as guides to action after a great deal of elaboration. A code of ethics which offers no clear resolution of major moral issues is unlikely to stand the test of providing any useful guidance in practice.

In part 4 we will attempt to construct a view of social work's ethical principles which overcomes the limitations of the idea of an ethical code. But first we need to turn to ethics' Siamese twin: politics.

3 The political in social work

In the claims of leader writers of some local newspapers, in the rhetoric of some conservative councillors and technocratically-minded social work managers, and in the words of some social workers themselves, one may readily see a strong disapproval of the notion that social work could, or should have anything to do with politics. Social work is seen as an individual service to people in distress; it should fulfil this function with efficiency, humanity and economy. Social workers should not meddle with political questions, for which they are not qualified, and which are beyond their proper concern. In what sense, then, has social work anything to do with politics? Is the pejorative and sceptical intent of these attitudes justified?

The idea of politics now has a very wide usage. Not only does it refer to the expressions of politicians and the actions of governments, but in everyday speech it extends to such areas as professional, or departmental, or local council politics. In addressing this distinction Raphael (1976, p. 27) states a preference for the old meaning that 'the political is whatever concerns the state', and suggests that the description of other areas of debate as political is metaphorical. Raphael's strict usage may be hard to maintain in current speech but it suggests a useful way of analysing the debate about politics in social work. It is argued here that social work is political in both the strict sense that it implies questions about the proper function of the state, and in the more colloquial sense of, for example, departmental politics.

Social workers in Britain and other western welfare democracies will hardly need to be reminded of the state's central role in the creation and maintenance of their agencies. By far the largest proportion of British social workers are employed directly by local government, which acts to fulfil the responsibilities assigned to it by the national legislature through statute: the enterprise of social work is an important component of Cockburn's (1978) 'local state'. The legislation is framed in wide and general terms, but is constantly refined and added to by quasi-statutory directives from central government. Its effects and priorities are modified by scandals, such as those surrounding child-abuse cases. Although in Britain most social work is administered by local government, recent experience has demonstrated again how the policies of local government may be negated by direct orders from central government. Even those relatively few social workers who are not employed by local government will probably be working for 'voluntary' agencies which are frequently dependent on government support in the form of grant aid or payment for services rendered. The voluntary social welfare agencies themselves are involved in a continual, if somewhat diffuse, dialogue about the boundaries of state responsibility for the welfare of individuals. If the state is to take responsibility for the prevention of child abuse – an assumption implicit in much current legislation – what is the role of the voluntary child protection agencies? The Lothian Region problem poses the question of the degree of state responsibility for income maintenance. If the state has arrogated the role of maintaining subsistence, under what circumstances ought the social work department – being another organ of the state – refuse to implement emergency measures for maintaining subsistence? Such examples are easily multiplied and underline the fact that the political involvement of the enterprise of social work is not merely adventitious, but intrinsic to it. Social work thus raises in a new context many of the classical problems of political theory which we have discussed in Chapter 3. However, the social work literature seems to propose no clear political philosophy or commitment of comparable importance to respect for persons in the area of personal morality. This topic will be taken up in Chapter 5 in a discussion of ideology.

Social work is, then, intimately involved with the political questions of the state proper. But the practice of social work also entails constant involvement with political action of a more domestic kind, where the focus of concern need not explicitly or necessarily be the state as such. This field of activity is not easily susceptible to exact definition; it shades off at one extreme into political questions of the sort referred to above, and at the other into localised intervention on behalf of individual clients undertaken in such a way as to have negligible political significance. Campaigns for social reform, local pressure group tactics, and any view of a social problem which emphasises its collective aspect, can all be construed as political action in social work. Lothian Region's response to the DHSS pay dispute must certainly be counted as political. Any demand for material resources on behalf of clients – for example, rehousing or pressing for welfare benefits – may involve the worker in activity which is political in the wider or more colloquial sense, such as appealing for the support of politically powerful individuals or resorting to confrontation when the basis for consensus-based negotiation ceases to exist. In the local authority context, the views of one political party against another, the demands of professional discretion versus the need for administrative accountability, the competing demands of alternative forms of provision, are all examples of political conflicts in the wider sense. The hallmark of 'domestic' politics in social work, which need not be overtly concerned with the organised state, the policies of its rulers or the ambitions of its opponents, is a concern with the power relationships affecting the parties to the intervention process. The issues involved will often be closely paralleled by questions of professional ethics, or, as in the case given at the beginning of this chapter, will be virtually indistinguishable.

This everyday political aspect then is scarcely avoidable, but the profession has traditionally been far more reluctant to embrace action on this level than it has been to justify its no less weighty involvement with individuals. Avoiding the term 'political', the BASW (n.d. – 1972?) Working Party on Social Action defended a concept in which 'social action comprises those aspects of social work and agency activity which have to do with promoting changes in the client's situation rather than in the client himself.' Social action was considered to be a supplement to, but not a substitute for, other ways of working. It remains a matter of general controversy whether any type of social intervention which gives explicit priority to the collective aspect – as in some forms of community work – is properly to be regarded as social work at all.

A further extension of the orbit of the political is seen in the now somewhat threadbare phrase 'the personal is political'. This viewpoint stresses that the personal problems individuals encounter in their daily lives within their circle of face-to-face contacts are products of wider political processes, and not just a reflection of the individual's own actions or inadequacies. Such a conception of the political is associated with a broadly Marxist position on the relationship between social structure and individual consciousness, but may also be held by conservatives.

The conclusion drawn from the preceding section was that social work is intrinsically a moral endeavour. This discussion points to a similar conclusion in respect of politics: social work is inescapably political. Moreover, not only does the general enterprise of social work bespeak the operation of certain policies and political philosophies, but the actions of individual social workers are very often intended to challenge or confirm the set of power relationships defining any given context where social work intervention is contemplated.

4 Social workers and the law

In the last chapter we saw that one of the key tasks of political theory is to account for the obligation to obey the law. We shall now portray, in the specific context of social work, a number of arguments which attempt to justify a moral obligation to obey the law. These considerations provide further evidence of the political involvement and implications of social work, as the legitimacy of laws is clearly a central question for political theory, and the content of laws a major feature of political programmes. We shall not expound the various theories in detail, but to illustrate the issues involved we shall consider a specific type of case in which social workers regularly face the question of whether, or why, they should be morally obliged to act in conformity with the law. In exploring the issues thus raised we shall have recourse to the traditional theories. It should be noted that it is primarily in the liberal tradition that political obligation appears as a central problem. This is because of the emphasis in liberalism on personal freedom, to which laws pose an obvious powerful threat.[2]

Under the provisions of the 1959 Mental Health Act a local authority social worker may be authorised, together with a medical practitioner, to commit a person to a mental hospital against his will. Can acting on this law, and thus apparently invading the person's moral and political rights, be justified? We shall consider the case where the worker believes that his action is morally justified, and disregard the possibility that he believes his action to be merely expedient and possibly unjustified. We may imagine that the social worker could present one of the following arguments.

(i) Contract view. In accepting citizenship of the state I have accepted an obligation to act in accordance with the law, and more specifically by undertaking the employment of social worker I have accepted an obligation to implement those laws for the carrying out of which social workers are entrusted with a special responsibility. In both the general responsibilities of citizenship and in the particular case of the social worker the obligation arises from a kind of contract between myself and other members of society, or alternatively with the state itself and through it the rest of society. In return for my adherence to the law, the state affords me legal status to protect my interests, defence from aggressors from within and without, and various economic and other benefits and privileges. Laws such as the 1959 Mental Health Act are necessary to preserve the harmonious functioning of society and it is therefore quite justifiable to remove a person's liberty, with proper safeguards, when the threat to himself or others is serious enough to warrant it.

It may be objected that hardly anyone nowadays makes a specific decision to accept citizenship; mostly it follows automatically from the accident of birth. Furthermore most people are not in a position to negotiate their contract with the rest of society, for similar reasons. Individual social workers are not really in position to enter negotiations about the content of the laws they are supposed to enforce. These are serious difficulties for the contract view. On the other hand it is possible to defend it by postulating that if the laws are in accordance with the position that the individual would have negotiated for himself had he in fact been free to do so, then the contract theory still makes an adequate basis for obeying the law.

(ii) Consent. A variant of the above argument would say that although I have had no opportunity to negotiate the particular privileges and costs of citizenship that apply in my society, nevertheless I demonstrate my support of them by consenting to them. This consent may be explicit but is more often tacit. Having given my consent to the laws, I am then morally bound to uphold them. In choosing to become a social worker I have in effect consented to the provisions of the Mental Health Act and so I am bound to implement it as occasion demands.

A major problem with the theory of consent is that it seems to imply a much broader scope for acceptance, by tacit agreement, than most people might willingly concede. If mere silence is to be interpreted as a promise it is hard to see how to avoid promises being imputed where they were never intended.

(iii) General will. As a social worker implementing the law I am reflecting and acting upon the will of the people as a whole. Thus, in our example, the legitimacy of depriving someone of his freedom under the Mental Health Act is derived from the fact that in our society this is the kind of treatment which is believed appropriate – it represents the values of society as a whole. It should not be assumed that the general will is necessarily identical with the wishes of the majority; rather, it represents something like the will of the whole social organism, whose own best interests are reflected in the positive actions of the state.

This view has a certain romantic appeal but is very hard to support by consistent rigorous analysis. If tenable, it does give a useful mandate to the social worker whose professional intervention may attract considerable disfavour from those immediately affected.

(iv) Common good. The point of obeying the law is simply that it is an effective way of maximising the common good. Thus, when I commit someone to mental hospital, the possible, and admitted, harm to his interests is outweighed by benefits to himself and those who may be affected by his deranged actions. Generally speaking, the laws are framed in such a way that obedience to them procures the common good, and so one's obligation to the state is not as a rule problematic. This utilitarian view has considerable commonsense appeal but contains some major difficulties. In common with a utilitarian approach to the morality of interpersonal relations, it asserts that the value of an action is to be assessed by the result obtained and therefore depends on a calculation of whose good is involved, and how much of it. Such a calculation is seldom straight-forward when we think it necessary to deprive someone of his liberty. It is also liable to disintegrate as a basis for a system of law if my calculation of what is conducive to the general good is different from yours: mine might lead me to obey the law, and yours to disobey. Now a system of law must be applicable consistently to all citizens if it is to be meaningful, but the utilitarian approach does not readily enable us to resolve different estimates of the common good. Some form of rule utilitarianism would seem to be the only defensible strategy.

(v) Justice. The purpose of the law is to create and uphold justice; indeed the legal system is often referred to as the system of justice. But justice is equally a central object of any system of morality. One can hardly imagine that an unjust system of social ethics could be defensible: it would, indeed, be an absurdity. If, then, committing someone to a mental hospital against his will is a just action then it should square with the demands of both personal morality and political obligation. The problem with this fairly crude argument will be evident from the discussion of justice in the previous chapter, where it was pointed out that it is not a unitary concept. In this example legal justice is confused with social justice, each of which may require different actions. Furthermore, the content of social justice is left unspecified. We have already commented on the tension in liberalism between rights and fairness concepts of social justice. Clearly, therefore, the idea of justice will not suffice as a ground of obligation without much fuller definition.

We have here briefly suggested certain lines of argument, derived largely from within the liberal tradition, which might explain the moral nature of the obligation to obey the law. It is also instructive to consider those cases where a social worker considers that in the course of his duties it is morally preferable to break or disregard the law. Take for example the social worker who, knowing that his client is engaged in some illegal activity, does not believe he ought to report the matter to the competent authorities. An instance of this involves the client who 'fiddles' his social security claim by making false declarations that enable him to claim more than his legal entitlement. Another instance is theft of electricity by interference with the meter. There can be little doubt that most social workers would regard it as unethical to report such happenings against the client's wishes. They could say that connivance is not the same thing as approval, and that there is no strict legal duty to report the offence. They might take the view that the principle of confidentiality precludes unauthorised disclosures. They might wish to point out to the client the error of his ways and persuade him to take steps to remedy the situation. Or they might condone the practice on the grounds that the low level of social security allowances is socially unjust anyway and the client is perfectly justified in playing the system for what he can get, or on the grounds that the cost of electricity is iniquitously high and the so-called theft amounts to no more than justifiable redistribution of resources. What these examples show is that the social worker's relation to the law is not a simple one whatever his views about its basis or the nature of the obligations it imposes.

5 Social science knowledge and social work praxis

The argument of this chapter has been that a politically and ethically neutral social work is impossible. The problem therefore becomes how to formulate a conception of social work which includes the ethical and political; ethics cannot be treated as an optional afterthought, nor politics as an irrelevant distraction. Now any conception of social work must give proper place to theory and knowledge and their relationship to practice, as well as to ethical and political considerations. We must therefore give some attention to the nature of social work theory.

The traditional approach to understanding the place of theory in social work practice sees the latter as resting on a knowledge base and a value base. The knowledge base comes from the social sciences and the value base from mainstream western moral values coupled with the specific requirements of a professional role. Siporin (1975), in his introductory textbook, develops this approach rather further than most. Drawing on the NASW model for social work practice, he sets out families of ethical and technical practice principles respectively. The ethical practice principles are based on the code of ethics, and the technical practice principles are derived from the social sciences. These are conjoined to give practice theory. In discussing similar topics Curnock and Hardiker (1979) attempt to distinguish between 'practice theory' – which would consist of a more sophisticated version of everyday practice wisdom – and 'theory for practice' which derives from the social sciences. This basic approach is typical of contemporary social work texts. It can also be traced in the formal requirements of social work courses. The received dogma wishes to assert simultaneously the importance of values in social work and its adherence to a scientific, rational body of knowledge. The pervasiveness of this 'practice = knowledge + values + skill' model (to put it rather simply) is perhaps remarkable in view of the increasing evidence[3] that social workers don't actually think in this way. That portion of the social science knowledge acquired in training which is subsequently re-tained mostly does not persist in the conventional codifications of the social sciences: rather, it is absorbed and reformulated in ways which shape the worker's understanding and actions without his being particularly aware of its disciplinary provenance. On the other hand 'practice theory' in social work is generally admitted to have attained only a rudimentary formulation, often not rising above the level of commonsense or maxim stated without justifica-tion ('start where the client is'). The persistence of the strait-jacket of official dogma is perhaps attributable to the dominance of positivistic conceptions of social science. In order to lend credibility to its claim to professional status, social work has needed the respectability of science, and the conception of science fastened on to for this purpose has been positivist. This is in spite of the paradoxical fact that it is problematic to reconcile at least one of the major traditions which have influenced social work, namely psychoanalysis, with positivism. According to the positivist view only knowledge securely grounded on empirical fact is worth enter-taining; anything intuitive, moral, spiritual or metaphysical must be regarded as unscientific or meaningless. And while the social sciences have made important progress in the last twenty years in disentangling themselves from the mesh of positivism,[4] social work has yet to benefit from this process. The relatively few writers in social work who have articulated a move away from positivism do not form a distinctive movement. At the same time formulations of social work practice theory, lacking any organic link with the social sciences, have remained stunted. The models offered in contempor-ary texts differ little in their framework assumptions from the initial formulations of Richmond's generation, even though their scope may have been extended beyond individuals in personal distress.

The predicament of social work theory could be summarised metaphorically in the following terms. Without a body of relevant social science knowledge, social work would have no map; and without a clear understanding of its purposes, social work would have no compass. But positivistic social science is the wrong map for social workers because the moral and spiritual dimension of relations between persons which is so clearly recognised in social work values is alien or even incomprehensible to the basic assumptions of positivistic social science. This science holds to the precept of being value free, but, as we have seen, social work cannot possibly be value free. The consequence seems to be that most social workers improvise their own map out of their own experience. It may serve them well enough, but it is hard to generalise this sort of guide into a recognised and validated scheme shared by the whole profession and amenable to improvement in each generation. It is this state of affairs which fuels the endless debates about the nature of social work.

The criticisms of social work theory being made here are, then, as follows: (i) it is inadequate in its own terms, (ii) its reliance on positivistic social science is out of sympathy with the intrinsically moral character of the nature of the enterprise to which social work is committed, namely the preservation or changing of parts of the social world, (iii) its traditional conception is not an accurate reflection of the way practitioners actually use their understanding of the problems they face, (iv) it is not properly connected to any recognisable general moral and political theory of the kind discussed in the last chapter. The first of these is not as radical as it may seem, for relatively few social workers of any tendency would claim that their body of professional knowledge has yet attained a high level of sophistication or comprehensiveness. The second criticism is supported by recent writing on the nature of social science. The second, third and fourth criticisms together point to the need for a conception which overcomes the characteristic splitting up of theory, values and action in the traditional view of social work. It will be proposed that the notion of *praxis* provides such a conception.

The idea of praxis has its roots in Aristotle and its most developed form in Marxism. Bernstein (1971) states Aristotle's doctrine as follows:

> Aristotle continues to use the expression in a general way to refer to a variety of biological life activities, but he also uses '*praxis*' to designate one of the ways of life open to a free man,

and to signify the sciences and arts that deal with the activities characteristic of man's ethical and political life (p. ix).

The end or *telos* of the practical disciplines or *praxis*, according to Aristotle, is not theoretical knowledge (although such knowledge is important for the practical disciplines). It is rather a distinctive type of activity . . . . The *telos* of the practical disciplines is to change our forms of activity and bring them into closer approximation to the full ideal of free human activity. However, for Aristotle, there is still a sharp distinction between the theoretical and practical disciplines, and philosophy as the study of first principles is a theoretical not a practical discipline (p. 316).

This approach suggests a way of escaping from the splitting up of theory, values and action. Social work is eminently a practical activity and even an art. It is clearly committed to the 'full ideal of free human activity', or in social work terminology, self-determination. And it must also embody some theoretical understanding, if it is not to result in mere caprice.

Bernstein traces four phases in the evolution of Marx's concept of praxis. (i) A man is what he does; the nature of man is determined by his praxis. In an alienated society the praxis and its products are alienated. (ii) Criticism of religion and philosophy must be extended to the real world of existing institutions, and this criticism given concrete expression as revolutionary practice. (iii) In *Capital* the idea of human activity as praxis is applied particularly to labour and its products as crystallised forms of labour. (iv) Revolutionary praxis leads to the overcoming of alienation and the realisation of man's true nature. The point here is epistemological – the diagnosis of man's condition as alienated is not a value judgement but a statement about social reality and man's potential.

The rich tradition of Marxism has, of course, debated these themes in considerable detail. The Marxian concept of praxis has been taken up and much amplified by the Frankfurt school of 'critical theory', represented by such writers as Marcuse and Habermas; their followers of the 'new left' have expressed an idealism which more radical social workers could find quite congenial. On the other hand the recent manifestation of a specifically Marxist social work literature has not given much attention to the potential of the concept of praxis and specially its epistemological impact. For as Bernstein remarks, both in Aristotle and in Marx the dogma of a dichotomy between questions of fact and questions of value – is and ought – is very much attenuated. Some hints of what this might imply for social work are to be found in the work of Freire, whose own debt to the Frankfurt school is clearly evident. Freire (1974) rejects the notion of education as the technical, value-free transmission of 'objectified' knowledge from teacher to student. The task of education is to *problematise* the actual living situation of learner and teacher: 'it is the antithesis of the technocrat's "problem-solving" stance' (1974, p. ix). The ideology of 'problem-solving' is indeed very prevalent in mainstream social work, and because it compartmentalises theory, method, and values, it is antithetical to praxis. For Freire, praxis comprises action and reflection. The want of action results in 'mentalism', and the want of reflection results in 'activism' (1972, p. 60); both are empty.

How then shall we conceive a praxis of social work? We have tried to show that abstracted social science knowledge and abstracted ethical principles are of limited value in informing one how to practise social work; they must first somehow be incorporated into each other. A praxis of social work must knit together a grasp of moral and political purpose, scientific and technical knowledge, and skilful performance in such a way that the end result demonstrates a necessary link with whatever first principles are elected. It is important also to recognise that none of these elements is logically prior to any other. Scientific knowledge is not a necessary precursor of skilful performance, nor is ethical behaviour necessarily a consequence of adopting certain abstract moral principles. Praxis means the all-round expression of its constituent elements, and as we have already implied there is much to suggest that social work is traditionally stronger in its actions than in its conceptualisations of them. To create a praxis, purpose, knowledge and skill must be pursued simultaneously and in relation to each other.

The approach we are advocating is by no means new to social work. Praxis principles – by which we mean conceptualisations of and for practice which give expression equally to the elements of knowledge, skill in performance, and moral purpose – exist in the mind of every social worker, even if in rudimentary form. But perhaps the best-known statement of such a set of principles is Biestek's (1961) classic text. In articulating seven principles of the casework relationship Biestek does not necessarily attempt to distinguish between the social scientific, the ethical and political, and the requirements of the purely practical; the principles in general embrace all three aspects, and fuse them together. Thus, for example, 'purposeful expression of feelings' may be understood as incorporating an ethical principle traceable to the concept of respect for persons. It also incorporates the psychological knowledge that people in distress are helped by being enabled to 'ventilate' their feelings to a sympathetic listener. And of course it is a common expectation that 'counsellors', in Halmos's (1978a) sense, should afford this opportunity to their clients. Biestek's work has perhaps lost something of its popularity as newer texts have attempted formulations more clearly adapted to circumstances in present-day social work agencies. The latter operate in different contexts, rest upon different assumptions and cover a much extended range of work as compared with what Biestek had in mind. The explicitly theological basis, the somewhat simplistic psychology and the lack of sociological perspective must all be discouraging to many readers. Changing expectations of the role of social workers have changed the emphasis of training courses, and no set of principles is likely to be valid indefinitely. But the outstanding merit of Biestek's approach is that it avoids the facile separation of the scientific and the ethical, which ultimately sterilises many social work texts. Biestek's principles are unmistakeably (though not always explicitly) social-scientific, moral-political, and practical at the same time; this, together with his clarity and relevance, accounts for his great influence.

We have already commented that much of social work's practice theory exists in only rudimentary form. It is surprisingly difficult to locate a substantial treatment of, for instance, 'starting where the client is' in the social work literature. The concept of praxis helps to explain that the practice theory of textbooks is not only or necessarily derived neatly by deduction from established social scientific knowledge. It may just as well be, and perhaps most often is, created by the actions and experiences of practitioners. Practice precepts of the 'start where the client is' variety have no meaning except as they can be grasped theoretically; and practice theory is empty except as it is translated into action.

Let us consider, purely for illustrative purposes, how the notion of a praxis principle might be applied to the Lothian Region problem. We have seen that social workers in different areas apparently took diametrically opposed courses of action; in some places they did give direct help to clients cut off from supplementary benefits, while in others they refused. If social workers adhere to a common body of praxis principles, this behaviour is at least paradoxical. One possible explanation is that the ruling principle for the direct-service workers was 'social workers should follow their agency's policies'. A justification could be constructed for such a principle taking into account its moral, political and technical aspects; such a justification might proceed along the following lines. It is also possible of course that the workers simply acted from expediency, and did not regard the policy as capable of satisfactory justification.

(i) Ethical aspects. The agency's policy satisfies the ethical canons of social work, such as respect for persons, self-determination, etc. This would imply that providing alternative financial support is not seen as the best way of following the precepts. Alternatively – if that seems far fetched – the duty to follow one's employer's instructions is of greater moment in this case than putative client needs.

(ii) Political aspects. This policy has been legitimately created by the appropriate agency acting with the legal authority derived from the democratic political process.

(iii) Technical aspects. This policy represents the considered opinion of senior members of the social work profession, who are in the best position to judge the practicality of alternatives.

Lest this 'justification' be misunderstood, let us repeat that it is not being advanced to defend (or condemn) the social workers' action – the aim is simply to illustrate the idea of a praxis principle. Whether social workers actually believe that following agency policy is the right way to practise is an empirical question. Nor is it our aim in this book to propose a complete or coherent set of praxis principles, which is the province of textbooks on practice. The essential point is the inseparability of the moral, political and technical aspects of social work, and the usefulness of the idea of praxis to bring these together in a manner which reflects how practitioners do their work.

One final point needs to be made to close this discussion. The range of issues that a social work praxis must address is extremely wide. Some are mentioned in the course of this book, but there are many others of great importance which might each very well constitute the subject of a separate enquiry. It is characteristic of these issues that they manifest themselves both as relatively mundane practical problems and as fundamental philosophical questions. A few examples will give an idea of the range and complexity. (i) How should a social worker deal with someone legally guilty of an offence which he, the social worker, does not believe is morally wrong? An example might be the use of certain drugs. (ii) On what basis should a social worker offer support and guidance to someone who holds opposed moral views to his own over the issue which has generated the social work involvement – for example, the possibility of abortion? (iii) Can it be justifiable to withdraw social work services in order to pursue the workers' self-interest, as in the case of strikes or other industrial action? (iv) What criteria and methods should be applied to ration services? Who should decide what type of service is made available? Considerations of utility and justice may well be in conflict here. (v) What principles should social workers use in deciding whether to give clients money? (vi) Social work involvement is often seen as stigmatising to the client. Does this matter? (vii) In what sense, if any, ought altruism to motivate professional social work?

It will be obvious that the arguments of this book do not in themselves aim to propose solutions to problems such as these. What we have attempted is to suggest some of the first principles that must be entailed in the effort to find solutions. In particular the concept of praxis emphasises the necessary relationship between theory and practice in social work.

Chapter five

Ideology in social work

1 The relevance of ideology

It has to be admitted that bringing ideology into a discussion of social work is almost asking for trouble. Social work already suffers enough from imprecise, ambiguous and misleading terminology; why add another term so dangerously loaded? But as Nathan Glazer (1968, p. 63) put it:

> *Ideology* is unquestionably one of those terms that, like *alienation*, might best be abandoned in serious discussion – if, that is, we did not need it so much, and if we could have any confidence that it would not return through the back door.

A passing acquaintance with the language of social work soon amply confirms that 'ideology' is alive (if not too well, perhaps) and ubiquitous. In this chapter we begin therefore by analysing the current meaning of the term, without being concerned with the history of the concept.[1] It is not our aim to associate particularly with the distinctive Marxist concept of ideology, which takes views on most of the issues denoted in the definition which follows. In the second part of the chapter we discuss a number of problems in the ideology of social work.

There are two major substantive concepts and various subsidiary meanings entailed in the term ideology. (i) An ideology is a set of political beliefs and values: for instance Fabianism or communism. In any plausible ideology the beliefs and values which it comprises will have a mutual consistency and complementarity stemming from their common basis in a small number of fundamental assumptions. Such a set of ideas prescribes the respective rights and obligations of the individual and the state; and at a more detailed level, policies to do with such matters as government intervention in economic activity, the control of crime, education, etc. (ii) An ideology is a conception of the nature and status of knowledge, especially about the social world: it identifies what is and is not to be counted as true knowledge.

Ideology has been used also to mean the science of ideas, and to refer to abstract speculation, but these meanings are becoming somewhat archaic. It is very important to realise that the two principal meanings are very closely related to each other. For the holder of an ideology, the proper course of action is self-evident to anyone with an unbiased view of the full facts. By defining what is to be counted as true and relevant, an ideology establishes the contours of the world in which the actor moves. At the philosophical level, moral and political values may be coupled to a view of true knowledge so as to produce a comprehensive scheme, or in the final analysis both the moral and epistemological questions may be unified in a grand system. A perennial philosophical problem is how to escape from the relativism that this notion of ideology brings; if all knowledge is ideological, it would seem that an objective, non-ideological understanding is impossible.

Besides its root meanings the term ideology carries a heavy weight of connotation and implication. (iii) To refer to someone's actions as being ideologically motivated may well be intended as derogatory or pejorative. It implies that he acted in the face of reason, or evidence, or commonsense, because his ideology gave him a distorted view of reality. Such accusations can usually be reciprocated. (iv) Supporters of ideological systems may make claims which tend to exceed the evidence they have to support them, at least in the eyes of the sceptic; or they may appeal to first principles which do not readily admit of proof or refutation. Hence adopting the system becomes at least in part a matter of faith. A socialist may claim that proper social arrangements should rule out large accumulations of personal wealth, while a conservative may counterclaim that personal property is not to be interfered with. These opinions depend on different estimates of the nature of social life and different value judgements which, however, are seldom made altogether explicit. Murdoch (quoted in Hunt, 1978, p. 18) describes man's pictures of himself as 'half a description, half a persuasion'. (v) Ideologies acquire motivating power; they inspire, prescribe and legitimate the goals men should aspire to. This is related to the element of faith mentioned above. Berger and Luckmann (1971, p. 141) say that 'ideologies generate solidarity'.

In Chapter 3 we proposed that political theories could broadly be classified into two camps, liberal and socialist. At this point it is necessary to state the relationship between political theories and ideologies. The essential point is simply that an ideology is a specific political philosophy adopted as a basis for action. An ideology does not rest with a purely analytical or theoretical stance to the problems of social life, but aims to translate the outcome of the theory into practical changes. When we speak of a socialist ideology we refer simultaneously to the values it adopts, the analysis it makes of their relationship and of the nature of social life, and the practical disposition to use this understanding as the basis for implementing a given social order. In the process of, and as a consequence of, adopting an ideology, it acquires the secondary significances listed above.

One further classification is useful in discussing ideology in the context of social work. In research into social service professionals and organisations a distinction has grown up between ideology in the general senses presented above, and what are variously termed 'operational philosophies' (Strauss et al., 1964, quoted in Smith, 1980), 'professional ideologies' (Giller and Morris, 1981), 'practice oriented ideologies' (Rees, 1978). Ideology in this latter sense – which for convenience we shall term practice ideology – refers primarily to those ideas, beliefs, theories, etc. which inform the professional's day-to-day work. The prescriptions that a practice ideology generates are therefore specific to the context to which they refer. This is in contrast to ideology in the general sense, which refers very broadly to principles for the whole of individual and social life. On the other hand it should not be assumed that any very firm distinctions can be maintained between general and practice ideology. A practice ideology must inevitably tend to reflect similar main premises and assumptions as its owner's general ideology. The ideal, perhaps, is for one's practice ideology to express in the context of professional work the same values and theories that one's general ideology embraces for life in general. Whether this is commonly achieved by social workers is another matter.

The relevance of the concept of ideology to social work is, then, that it is a convenient, and moreover inescapable, way of referring to the combination of social value, analysis and action which social work entails. It follows from the foregoing discussion that to see social workers as possessing an ideology does not represent an evaluative statement but a descriptive one. Every rational person possesses some sort of ideology, and its possession is a different matter from whether it is a good or a bad ideology. The complexity of the concept is a useful reminder of the many assumptions that are made, explicitly or implicitly, every time a piece of social work is carried out. To understand someone's ideology is to grasp his view of the world and some of his motivations for pursuing his projects. To integrate the constituent elements of one's own ideology is arguably essential to practising with integrity.

It will be apparent too that many key concepts in social work including those discussed in this book are ideologically loaded: that is to say that they are seldom employed as straightforward descriptive epithets, but also imply and evoke a certain understanding of social reality and certain evaluations. Thus, for example, self-determination implies among other things philosophical libertarianism and the adoption of a certain concept of liberty. It is extremely important to be aware of the ideological potential inherent in much social work language; much of it is too often overlooked.

The concerns of this chapter may now be linked to the arguments which have just preceded it. Ideology and praxis are, in effect, two sides of the same coin. Both concepts necessarily invoke morals, politics, and one's understanding of the nature of knowledge and action. Specifically, a social worker's praxis bespeaks his ideology; he gives concrete expression to his practice ideology in his practice. The value of the concept of praxis is that it avoids the compartmentalisation of value, knowledge, theory and skill, and looks upon these interrelated activities as a whole. The point of referring to ideology is that it links the minutiae of practice to broader conceptions of knowledge and of social and moral value.

Many controversies in social work turn around interesting and important ideological differences. Or rather, it would be more precise to say that ideological debates have important manifestations as different approaches to practice; because praxis and ideology reflect different aspects of the same social reality.

Although we have defined ideology and praxis as occupying a reciprocal relationship, this now needs a note of qualification. Social workers, like everyone else, may make statements of which the ideological content is at variance with their actual practice: they may believe one thing, say another, and do something else. We do not suppose that social workers are any more susceptible to misplaced rationalisation, unfounded conjecture, misinformation, bad faith, herd instinct, or self-delusion than other people; in pointing to the disparity we simply note a general phenomenon. However, it follows from the concept of praxis that a person or group's ideology is not to be identified merely from what they say, but from the totality of their action, including their words. A theoretical ideology is, in effect, only half an ideology and should not be mistaken for the whole.

In the remainder of this chapter we shall discuss a number of ideological tensions in social work. These are mostly at the level of general ideology as it directly affects practice ideology. Incidentally we shall recapitulate a number of themes previously discussed in this book. There will be good reason to recall Pearson's (1975a, p. 130) comment: 'ambiguity asserts itself at every point in professional culture.' For the content of theoretical ideologies we refer to the literature. Reliable empirical information on social workers' ideologies is scanty and uneven, and for our present purpose we must be satisfied if we can raise the most important issues.

2 Ideological tensions in social work

(a) Radical social work?

The banner of radical social work provides a reference point for many social workers uneasy about the possible contradictions between, on the one hand, the personal and political values they wish to actualise in their work and, on the other, what they fear are the retrograde tendencies endemic to the organisations that carry out social work. It seems very probable that the criticisms which have been explicitly voiced by self-consciously radical social workers are shared to some extent by a substantial segment of the profession who do not make any overt commitment to the radicals' camp. There is a close affinity between the radicals' critique of social work and mainstream views of what social work exists to, and does, achieve, and the differences between them are perhaps more of degree than of kind. The radical faction is by no means a homogeneous group any more than is the body of non-radical social workers, and the distinction between them is far from sharp.

It is not self-evident what radical means in this context. In her book *Radicals in Social Work*, Statham (1978) adopted a rather clumsy distinction between 'liberal radicals' and 'left radicals'. Strictly speaking the term 'radical' must be applicable to any ideology which departs in fundamental terms from that which is generally held in a given social unit; for example radicalism can be from left or right of the political spectrum. Now liberalism can certainly not be regarded as an extreme doctrine in societies which sustain social work and thus the notion of 'liberal radical' seems (at least in Britain) self-contradictory. In the culture of social work, radical connotes a link with socialism; and as socialism is an extremely broad tendency, so is the range of opinion to be found amongst radical social workers. Statham's liberal and left radicals represent different shades of socialism. Radical social work may briefly be characterised as follows:

(i) A commitment to some variety of socialism, varying in colour from mild social reformism to revolutionary Marxism. In this view social problems arise primarily from a specific societal context rather than from the failings of individuals; it is the social system which requires change, not the individuals who are unfortunate enough to incur the results of defective social arrangements.

(ii) A mistrust of the authority with which the social worker's role is imbued, deriving from his legal responsibilities, administrative and class status and professional power. Professionalism is, at least, suspect; authentic personal relationships between client and worker are preferable to relationships of instrumental authority. Status differentials between client and worker ought to be reduced or eliminated. The social control function which most social work is believed to embody is seen as antipathetic to larger ideological goals.

(iii) A commitment to participatory styles of decision-making, within and between agencies and as between social worker and client. Bureaucratic exigencies are an impediment. Hence the worker may have to fight his own agency as well as external obstacles to fruitful change.

(iv) Doubt about or disaffection with the nuclear family as the basic social unit, and an aspiration to other forms of social living such as the collective or the community. This is a corollary of a partial or total rejection of the ethic of individualism which is seen to underlie social work and western society in general. Doubt about the nuclear family contrasts with current political thinking on the right, which seeks a return to a traditional conception of family life.

It should be clear that this sketch does not itself provide a viable account of how radical social work is, or could be, practised; but it shows that the idea of radical social work presents formidable practical and theoretical difficulties. What is the correct socialist analysis? How can any social worker meaningfully sustain the role in the light of an analysis that fundamentally criticises the system which, in effect, defines his occupational role? How may one distinguish the social problems attributable to the system from the signs and causes of human distress (such as illness, grief, scarcity) which must be assumed to arise in any utopia? Dilemmas such as these permeate the writings on radical social work and one can only conclude that the case for a radical social work has not yet been made out. It is therefore debatable whether or not radical social work is actually a contradiction in terms; social work as it is, and conceivably could be, practised may be fundamentally inconsistent with the tenets of radical social work. The issues, however, are not less important because of that: radical or not, any social work engenders similar ones. Radical social workers evince disillusion with social work as it is currently practised, and sometimes even with their own faith. They may also be deluded, if radical social work turns out to be founded on a series of misunderstandings and no radical praxis is possible. As a theoretical ideology, however, radical social work is a significant force, and it also provides an excellent illustration of some of the ideological conundrums that infect all social work. The issues raised by radical social work are close enough to the mainstream of practice to be pertinent to social workers of all persuasions, even though all may not agree with various of the radicals' premises.

(b) Social work and social change

In the history of social thought there have been markedly different views on the need, or otherwise, for purposive intervention in social affairs. At one extreme Adam Smith's invisible hand is seen as ensuring optimal social arrangements through individuals pursuing their own enlightened self-interest; deliberate attempts to bring about social change are neither necessary or desirable. With its association with the economic doctrine of laissez-faire this view has been of well-known importance historically. Although absolutist adherence to this opinion is rare in this era of the mixed economy, it has left a powerful legacy of suspicion of interventionism. George and Wilding (1976) characterise Keynes, Beveridge and Galbraith as 'reluctant collectivists' who would much rather prefer to avoid state intervention, but were obliged to admit that the disastrous consequences of unregulated capitalism required judicious mitigation. At the other extreme are those theories, especially communism, which hold that the existing social order is fundamentally destructive of human fulfilment and must therefore be deliberately broken down to make way for the new. Some would prefer to focus their attention on the quality of interpersonal relationships rather than large-scale societal issues, and see alienation and false consciousness as problems to be tackled at the level of ordinary daily life.

While the conservative impulse (Marris, 1974) is often associated with the political right and the urge to reform with the political left, it is a mistake to assume that the left-right polarity is synonymous with the concern with social change. The radical right shares with the radical left a dislike of the existing social order, though of course the specific content of the critique is different in either case. Nozick (1974) has presented a case for dismantling most of the existing state apparatus. Recent conservative governments in the UK and USA wish to introduce changes no less sweeping than those proposed by their leftist opponents.

Social conflict entails a high price, and radical programmes of whatever sort must face this. It would not be surprising if radicals wished, for tactical reasons, to remove from prominence the personal and social costs of bringing about the changes they desire; but revolutionaries are not so squeamish. Reformers of a milder persuasion hope they can achieve the changes they wish without too

107

high a price in anguish, disruption or violence. Radicals of the left hold a theory of society which stresses the intrinsic nature of conflict, especially between social classes, in the understanding of social relations; an alternative view of the radical right might emphasise the essentially conflictual nature of relations between individuals. Reformers are more inclined to see society as better explained by a consensus view of social relationships.

The tension between whether the need is for positive intervention to produce social change, or whether it is best to let things alone, is readily seen in social work. Extreme non-interventionism is probably incompatible with social work, which seeks change in different social systems at various social levels. And yet social work is extremely ambivalent about the extent to which intervention is desirable. In the discussion of self-determination and paternalism we traced opposing tendencies in the commitment of social work: on the one hand, a belief in planned change associated with a positive concept of freedom; on the other, a hankering for a strong doctrine of self-determination associated with a negative concept of freedom.

As regards its prevailing ideology, it is widely held that social work is concerned with change – however varied or obscure may be the understanding of the specific character of that change. We wish now to put forward the thesis that social work is much better characterised by its concern for preserving the social order and that any changes it may bring about are more like the processes observed when a disturbed homeostatic system returns to equilibrium. Change is not the same as movement, which may simply return one to the point whence one came.

A number of arguments could be put forward to support the view that social work really is concerned to achieve change. These include (i) the characteristic area of activity of social workers is that of psycho-social functioning, or in other words each individual's mediation of the external, social demands of the world and his own inner drives, desires and feelings. In aiming to get a better fit between inner and outer worlds the social worker may either do something about the social situation, such as gain access to additional resources for the client, or do something about the client's psychological adjustment by counselling, or very probably do both together. The effect of the worker's intervention is to bring about change in the client's outer or inner worlds, or their mutual relationship. (ii) A second argument would be that it is part of the social work task to bring about changes in the policies and practices which tend to give rise to the problems that social workers have to deal with, such as poverty, homelessness, and cultural deprivation. Social reform constitutes a valid and necessary facet of social work.

We think that these arguments are short sighted. Change is a relative matter – it has to be in relation to something. From the point of view of individual worker and client there can be no doubt that something usually happens in association with the worker's involvement, even if the relationship between what is intended and what is achieved seems frequently to be far from predictable or straightforward. However, social work cannot adequately be described merely by the sum of transactions between workers and clients: it has to be seen in its societal context. From this point of view there is little to support the position that social work promotes significant social change. Social workers are expected to uphold prevailing social values and social work therefore acts to promote the preservation of several centrally important institutions, among them the family, the close link between status and employment, and the social values embodied in the criminal justice system. In his contact with the poor the social worker is not expected to enable the client to address the structural origins of poverty in capitalist society. In dealing with the deviant the worker is expected to correct the deviant behaviour rather than to change the norms which define the behaviour as deviant. The meagre social reforms brought about by social work are small in relative terms, and it is more realistic to see them as marginal adjustments than major changes. This is not merely because social work may lack the political power to bring about substantive changes, but arises from the more fundamental reason that the ideology of social work does not in fact seek real social change. The claim that social work is concerned with change is perhaps best understood as deriving from another aspect of social work ideology, its preoccupation with the individual, which we discuss below.

(iii) A third argument in favour of the view that social work is concerned with change has a different starting point. This is the radical's claim that, even if social work as we know it must be admitted to be rather ineffective in promoting change, nevertheless it is its proper function to do so. On this ideology the task is to devise a form of practice which will actively promote real social change. We have already commented that the case for the possibility of a radical social work has still to be made out; this ideology has still to find a praxis, and current writing suggests that its exponents still have far to go. The radical view calls for major changes in precisely those institutions which social work as we know it seeks to preserve. It seems doubtful therefore that any enterprise dedicated to those ends of change could count as social work at all.

(c) Social work for one and all

Social work has always been conscious of its supposed dual obligation to 'individual' and 'society'. This dichotomous presentation obviously reflects a gross oversimplification; any analysis must begin from a recognition that individual and society are concepts that cannot be understood alone, but only in relation to each other. It is a truism that society consists ultimately of individuals, and equally that individuals are necessarily products of their society. Without the social collectivity, human personality could not be formed; and without human beings, human society is obviously impossible. Nevertheless the baldly stated individual-society problem does serve to remind us of a crucially important characteristic of social work. In many, perhaps most, occupations the worker's primary accountability is reasonably clearly defined; the industrial worker to his boss; the dentist, estate agent, engineer and so forth to his client; the public servant to the bureaucracy which employs him. Social work however shares with a number of other occupations an aggravated problem of loyalty: it cannot adequately define its allegiance except by stressing the multiplicity of that allegiance. No social work is conceivable that does not necessarily involve multiple, and very possibly conflicting, loyalties. If a social worker is asked to arrange residential accommodation for a mentally or physically infirm old person, he may have to try and reconcile the old person's repugnance at the idea, the family's inability to continue maintaining their relative in the community, and the rival demands of other old people in a similar situation. If a social worker is asked to prepare a court report on a juvenile offender he may face the likelihood that no available disposal may be of much use in alleviating the predisposing factors that led to the offence. If a social worker encounters a child who may be at risk of non-accidental injury, he must decide whether the potential risk to the child justifies his agency's intrusion upon the presumed right of the family to live without interference from local government officials. And so on: the point is that these conflicts are not merely unfortunate difficulties that crop up in isolated cases, but are intrinsic to social work.

One way to avoid such dilemmas over loyalty is simply to deny their existence and substitute an ideology which defines where the worker's loyalty should lie. In the epoch of the Charity Organisation Society the worker's aim required discrimination between those whose poor circumstances could be attributed to unkind fate and who could be helped by strategic aid, and those who had to be blamed for their behaviour. The thrust of the worker's effort was decided according to whether the client was deserving or undeserving. In this view the obligation to society to control the menace of pauperism is dominant. A contrasting view which drew its inspiration from social work's entanglement with psychoanalysis emphasised as the primary focus of the worker's attention the intrapsychic stresses to which the client's problems were traceable; social distress was fundamentally the individual's own problem and the worker must concern himself with that and not get involved in irrelevant political issues. A third view, rather strongly associated with radical social work and community work, sees individuals' problems as manifestations of societal problems. Chief among these are poverty, considered to result from structural inequalities in the distribution of resources, and the very closely related problem of political powerlessness. Hence the proper sphere for relieving social distress is some form of political action.

Now, these are caricatures, and in this crude form cannot long be defended in serious analysis; there must be qualifications and corrections. Nonetheless there is evidence to suggest that social workers do fall back on suchlike simplifications to enable them to steer a course through the ambiguities noted by Pearson. But in doing so they are denying the issues, not resolving them.

As social work in Britain has become progressively absorbed into the local state, so has the range of responsibilities it is expected to undertake diversified and multiplied. The narrow remit of the pre-reorganisation agencies for child care, welfare, and mental health was replaced in England and Wales by the Seebohm concept of comprehensive community-based personal social services. In part this implied joining together to eliminate gaps and overlapping between them, inefficiencies, and shortage of resources. But beyond that, the new community based service was to be

> directed to the well being of the whole community and not only of social casualties, and seeing the community it serves as the basis of its authority, resources and effectiveness. Such a conception spells, we hope, the death-knell of the Poor Law legacy and the socially divisive attitudes and practices which stemmed from it. (Seebohm, 1968, para. 474)

In Scotland the government's proposals (SED/SHHD, 1966, paras 12–17) for social service reorganisation emphasised the central role of the new social work department in planning for the wellbeing of the whole community. In practice it would appear that the heavy costs of reorganisation and the growing burden of responsibilities have tended to overshadow aspirations to increase the range and multiply the targets of the personal social services (Satyamurti, 1981; DHSS, 1978); certainly it cannot be claimed that the concept of a comprehensive community service has generally been realised. But the ideology of a community-oriented service is very much alive and has lately received fresh impetus in the context of proposals for patch systems (Hadley and McGrath, 1980) which make explicit efforts to involve ordinary members of the community in providing the care which social workers have tended to see as their responsibility. In a recent book Hadley and Hatch (1981) criticise the failure of the state-controlled social welfare apparatus to deliver what has been expected of it, and advocate a decentralised, community-based approach relying less on professionals' own direct work. The recent proposals of the Barclay Committee (1982) attach great importance to the social worker as one who arranges and organises social care, rather than providing it directly himself.

The ideology of a comprehensive community service seems to imply considerable audacity: it seems almost to amount to the claim that social work is in some way responsible for the material and moral welfare of everyone, everywhere. If social workers are the new secular priesthood the claim has a certain logic but loses none of its stupendousness. It is little wonder that the approach has been criticised for its lack of relevance and drawn forth pleas for a return to a limited conception of social work.

The foregoing selection of issues illustrates that social work evidently faces in particularly acute form the ancient problems of conflicting obligations to individual and society. Now despite the conceptual and material interdependence of these two areas of concern, the habit of focusing on one or the other is deeply ingrained in western thinking. In its positive aspect this leads to a fruitful dialectic on how the respective claims of individual and society are to be reconciled, but it may lapse into a disastrous split vision. Pearson (1975a, p. 129) criticises social work for its ambiguity as to 'what kind of place this abstract "individual" has in this reified "society".' What do social philosophy and social science have to say to enable one to avoid the dangers of split vision?

The disciplines of moral and political philosophy tend to address the individual-society problem from the perspective of one or the other respectively. In commenting on this relationship Joad (1938) argues that the ancient Greeks regarded morals and politics as simply two different aspects of the same set of problems. But the influence of Christianity, with its central preoccupation with individual salvation, diverted attention away from politics on to the area of right conduct for the individual. As a result political philosophy was eclipsed until the Renaissance. In the last two hundred years there has been a rapprochement as philosophers have recognised the inevitable interdependence of morals and politics, and in the twentieth century they are once again joined. Despite this historical parting, many of the classic issues in moral and political philosophy revolve largely around the individual-society problem, as was evident in Chapter 3.

A distinctive focus on the needs of either the individual or the community is clearly visible in the commitments of political parties. This is the primary distinction between the political left and right. The right stresses the freedom of the individual from unnecessary or excessive state interference and the protection of individual interests within a strong framework of law; the role of the state should be kept to the unavoidable minimum necessary for its continued preservation. The left prizes substantive equality and fellowship; it is less tolerant of individual deviations from the common social purpose. A comprehensive state is necessary to pursue its objectives.

In the arena of social science C.W. Mills's famous distinction between private troubles and public issues is once more concerned with whether we should look to individual or society for an understanding of social problems:

> *Troubles* occur within the character of the individual and within the range of his immediate relations with others; they have to do with his self and with those limited areas of social life of which he is directly and personally aware . . . . *Issues* have to do with matters that transcend those local environments of the individual and the range of his inner life . . . . An issue is a public matter: some value cherished by publics is felt to be under threat. (1970, p. 15)

Mills appealed for a sociological imagination which would transcend the narrow and distorted vision that apprehends only troubles or only issues. His aim (and his achievement) was at once intellectual and practical, scientific and moral; it was very much a praxis.

Mills's distinction between troubles and issues represents a fruitful way of looking at the individual-society problem because it both recognises the very real tensions that the question generates and it emphasises how the two aspects are fundamentally inseparable. It is an effective yardstick for assessing ideologies in social work; no modern-thinking, generically trained social worker can fail to feel nettled by Mills's (1970, p. 100) judgement of social workers (and others) that 'their professional work tends to train them for an occupational incapacity to rise above a series of "cases".' However broad may be the social work task envisaged by those who speak for the profession at a high level of generality it is hard to resist the impression that most social workers actually practise in a way that reflects the prominence in their minds of either the personal troubles or the public issues: and Mills's claim amounts to the dominance of the personal troubles. The leading ideology of community work, on the other hand, attaches priority to public issues, and this contrast of views very largely accounts for the ambivalent relationship between mainstream social work and community work. Accepting the perspective of Mills's sociological imagination, it can be seen that trading insults on the relative merits of social work and community work is futile. Anyone who wants to achieve social change must understand both history and biography.

The ideological axis between individual and society reappears in social work as a family of rough dichotomies that can be grouped under the heading of the personal and the political. Should social workers concentrate on helping individual cases or achieving political reforms? Is social work about caring for the deprived and disadvantaged, or controlling the deviant? Are social problems traceable to poverty and material deprivation, or to psychological maladjustment? By now it should be clear that rough disjunctions of this sort are untenable. Halmos (1978b) was absolutely right to insist on the necessity of maintaining a sort of creative tension between such possibly competing interests.

It would certainly appear that the contemporary ideology of social work is very much inclined to the perspective of the individual; Mills's charge does not seem to have lost much of its force. From a historical point of view, social work has its roots in Christianity and classical liberalism, both of which give pride of place to the concept of the autonomous individual; although under heavy attack, these ideologies must still be regarded as dominant. In terms of the values social work embraces, we have discussed the centrality of respect for persons, which naturally directs one's view to the position of the individual rather than the needs of the social collectivity. The literature proposes nothing in the political sphere so readily identifiable as respect for persons in the personal sphere.

It might be objected that no modern conception of social work is so narrow. Any standard textbook refers to the place of social work between individual and society. Developments in British social work since the late 1960s, such as those reflected in the Seebohm and Barclay reports, give considerable emphasis to a community-based service for community needs. But these developments tend to conceal a hidden value orientation in favour of the individual. The point of community-based services is usually to facilitate better methods of helping individuals who might alternatively have been aided by a direct professional service. Whatever the rhetoric, it does not seem to be the aim in practice to provide services to reach those who wouldn't have needed professional intervention anyway.

The dominance of the ideology of respect for persons conceals a paradox in social work's orientation to individual or community.

Social workers have always accepted, albeit with some reluctance, that their work implies elements of social control; that it is an inevitable part of the role to demand and enforce compliance with social norms. The specific character of these norms changes over time, but not the position of the social worker in having to enforce them. This is seen very obviously in for example statutory child care, probation and mental health. The social control element is, however, far more pervasive than even these broad categories would imply. In every relationship of social worker and client, the help sought and offered is mediated by a set of assumptions on either side concerning what is actually or potentially available, and what is and is not appropriate on practical and moral grounds. The relationship is never purely a technical transaction or an instrumental means to an end: it is 'socially constructed' (Berger and Luckmann, 1971). Now social workers in general occupy a position of greater status and power than their clients, and it is therefore the construction which the social worker makes of the boundaries and content of the client-worker relationship which will tend to predominate. To a large extent the worker imposes the morality he adopts, either on his own behalf or on behalf of some larger collectivity, upon the client. This leads us to expect that the element of social control will be all-pervasive and inevitable. The following examples illustrate the point. In helping a client to extricate himself from debt, the social worker affirms and reinforces the social and legal conventions which demand that poor people pay a high proportion of their income for necessities such as fuel and housing; or in arranging residential accommodation for a frail elderly person, the social worker endorses the opinion that the responsibility for caring should be assumed by the state.

The paradox in social work's orientation to individual and society may now be stated as follows. On the one hand, we have the dominance of the individualist theoretical ideology of respect for persons. On the other hand, when we examine the typical praxis of social work, we find that it is massively involved in social control such that the full implications of respect for persons are liable rapidly to be put out of reach by the exigencies of the professional role which social workers adopt. The case of Lothian Region given in the last chapter exemplifies the problem. We may well then ask whether it is not the dominance of societal, and not individual, needs which best explains the praxis of social workers.

(d) Technique or encounter?

The official view of social work, articulated in any number of textbooks and endorsed by the professional organisations and accrediting bodies, is absolutely clear that practice should rest upon a foundation of social science knowledge. In this respect social work is seen as similar to other professions which command access to a body of specialised knowledge. It is of course admitted that the knowledge base is as yet rather imperfectly developed, but the ideal remains of a steadily growing and ever more powerful social-scientific corpus whose application is necessary to and even definitive of good practice. Social work courses therefore teach sociology, psychology, social administration and other academic disciplines considered useful. Somewhere between these academic disciplines and the realities of actual practice lies the nebulous region of 'practice theory' which is admittedly even more imperfectly developed than the academic disciplines. However, a rapidly growing literature is emerging to try and fill this gap.

The scientific approach is compatible with the once-popular division of social work into several methods – casework, group work, community work and, latterly, residential work. The various methods were seen as drawing from specific areas of social science knowledge. More recently this rather constricting framework has been overhauled and replaced by an emphasis on the flexible application of different techniques according to the task in hand. But whatever the social science content thought relevant, the common factor has been a belief that good social work depended on the careful application of scientific knowledge.

Buried just below the surface of the ideology of scientific social work lies the belief in some kind of social engineering; that techniques for understanding and intervening in people's lives can be developed by the same kind of controlled manipulation that has led to man's overwhelming of the natural environment. In social work there is a persistent though arguably ill-founded ambition to affect general social conditions by similar means. For the most part this manipulation is benign, and even philanthropic, in intent, even if its effectiveness is still somewhat provisional. But for all the dominance of the scientific ideology, social work perennially harbours a doubt about its relevance and validity. The most primitive manifestation of doubt is the belief of a good many sceptical outsiders – and not a few social workers – that all that is required to do social work is sincerity, commonsense, and a knack for getting on with people. Then there is the quaint but explicit claim that the most important thing a social worker can offer is his relationship with the client, defined as a good in itself. Firmly established in the mainstream culture of social work is the notion that the social worker's 'use of self' is a vitally important skill. Unfortunately this doctrine is not well founded on any explicit statement of what constitutes the self, and is therefore difficult to interpret. Also within the mainstream is the concept of a one-to-one counselling relationship where carefulness, respect, an individualised, personal approach, an intuitive grasp of the other's situation, and empathy are all vital characteristics. These concepts are readily identified with the principle of respect for persons which, as we have argued, is indispensable to the definition of social work. However, in stressing the significance of the personal encounter, such approaches seem to be at variance with the scientific ideology. At any rate it is not easily apparent why respect for persons and the scientific ideology should be expected to coexist in the same praxis, as the 'practice = knowledge + values + skill' model commonly holds.

A number of social work writers have doubted the scientific ideology, and a few have explicitly rejected it. Wilkes (1981) has argued against the obsession with method in social work and proposed that the quest for technical effectiveness obstructs the realisation of an authentic, appreciative relationship between client and worker, particularly for those 'undervalued groups' – such as the elderly and the handicapped – whose predicament does not admit of a technical solution. In somewhat similar vein Ragg (1977) rejects the concepts of diagnosis and treatment, favouring a strong conception of human agency and personhood and a personal rather than an instrumental client-worker relationship. The ideology of these writers challenges some of the basic premises of establishment social work; in effect they question not just the relative merits of different approaches to an agreed conception of social work, but its essential nature. They bring to the surface problems of the relationship of fact and value, knowledge and meaning, being and knowing, subjectivity and objectivity, which are too often disregarded in the official ideology.

We see then that the tension between the scientific and the intuitive, technique or encounter, raises problems about the basis of knowledge as well as those of social value. It should be remembered that ultimately the contrasts we are investigating in this chapter are not independent of each other; one's views about knowledge and one's social values must in the end rest upon the same fundamental logical and metaphysical assumptions if some kind of consistency is to be maintained. The area of study known as meta-ethics is concerned with the questions of meaning which must be clarified in order to support the normative whose object is to prescribe conduct. Indeed, for much of this century English-speaking philosophers have been more interested in meta-ethics than normative ethics. In political philosophy as in ethics one cannot proceed very far without making some assumptions about the nature of man; for example any theory about the proper function of the state must inevitably take into account the nature of the being for whom the arrangements are being propounded. To a certain extent therefore moral and political philosophy rest upon assumptions which are psychological or sociological in character. But we are concerned here with a different sort of question, which might initially be expressed as: how do you know that your psychological and socio-logical premises are properly founded? How, for example, can you defend the claim that man's essential nature is to seek his own immediate gratification? This type of question eventually shifts the enquiry away from the sociological or psychological plane to the level of the basis of knowledge – how do you know that you know? Evidence and argument in support of such a proposition would be examined not only by the normal criteria of accuracy, self-consistency, validity and so on, but also for the kind of usually unspoken assumptions that inform the choice of evidence and the weight which attaches to it. As we commented earlier, part of the function of an ideology is to define what counts as 'true' knowledge.

The problem of how to account for, and justify, one's methodol-ogical assumptions in studying man or indeed any other phe-nomenon has been a matter of fierce debate in recent years. The newcomer to this field could well be put off by a hail of 'isms', often expressed in opposing pairs: empiricism – rationalism, positivism – humanism, materialism – idealism, and so on. Perhaps even more alarming is the discovery that many of these terms are apt to mean different things in the hands of different authors. We shall not enter into these debates here except in the very limited way we indicate below. But it needs to be borne in mind that some sort of grasp of the issues about the foundations of social science is essential to a critical understanding of research in social work and thus of social work's aspiration to improve its effectiveness by means of a scien-tific approach to practice.

The single aspect of the problem of how to set about understand-ing social reality which we wish to remark upon can roughly be stated as follows. On the one hand, a positivist view: the methods of the natural sciences have demonstrated outstanding success in advancing our knowledge of the natural world and hence may be taken as authoritative. A corollary is the assumption that man may differ in degree of complexity from other creatures, but not in kind. Therefore a proper application of scientific method to the study of man will provide the best – or only – path to true knowledge. On the other hand, a humanist view: man differs from other organisms in certain fundamental respects, notably in having the capacities of rationality and self-understanding. The methods of the natural sciences cannot take account of these characteristics and are there-fore inapplicable. Furthermore, the traditional conception of the natural sciences is inadequate even for understanding those sciences themselves, because (inter alia) it fails to take account of the fact that science itself is a social product.

It should be apparent that the opposition here is rather closely analogous to the debate between libertarianism and determinism which we discussed in Chapter 1. We commented there on the paradox resulting from social work's claim on the one hand to the libertarian doctrine of respect for persons, and on the other to its adherence to determinist scientific theories as the basis for professional intervention. For the social worker who makes any pretence to be guided by knowledge and method there exists a similar opposition between the positivist and humanist views of human nature. We have already commented that in the official view positivism seems clearly to have the upper hand, but that the culture of social work is in many ways profoundly humanist.

We do not have the scope here to examine the virtues of these rival opinions, or attempt a resolution of them, but refer the reader to fuller discussions elsewhere.[2] Within the context of our present discussion of ideologies in social work, we simply wish to emphasise that a social worker's ideology must be traced not only with reference to his social and political values, but also to his beliefs about how a true understanding of man and the social world are to be arrived at. Social work can no more avoid epistemological and ontological problems than it can moral and political ones.

(e) Practice ideologies

Our discussion in this chapter has mostly turned on general ideologies, which are concerned with very broad questions of social value and the basis of knowledge. Much of the ground is equally relevant to a large range of other activities than social work. To conclude, we must ask what link can be made with practice ideologies in social work.

The social work literature does contain a large amount of material which is ideologically prescriptive; the literature of community work probably contains proportionately much more. The extent to which all this is put into practice is, of course, a different question which must be studied empirically. Much recent research into social work, especially if influenced by the interpretive tradition in sociology, sheds light on social work ideologies. In some cases ideology has been adopted as a central concept in the design and interpretation of research. We shall mention two examples of this. Rees identified a 'general ideology of helping' in the social workers he studied, and within that, three practice-oriented ideologies. The 'casework' ideology was identified by 'the assumption that certain people could and should be helped through the medium of interpersonal relationships' (Rees, 1978, p. 54). In the 'service' ideology the emphasis was on immediate practical benefits, especially for the old or disabled. Thirdly the ideology of 'relief' 'conceptualises what action was considered open to [the social workers] once they regarded people as having difficulties related to the source and size of their income' (p. 57).

Smith (1980) took a somewhat different but not incompatible approach in his study of social workers' ideologies of need. He identified three dimensions for distinguishing ideologies of need: the unit of need (individual, family or community); the causes of need (material shortage, psychological inadequacy, or moral weakness); and the definition of who should act as the assessor of need (professional social worker, referral agent, or client).

The empirical evidence for social workers' ideologies is far from complete, but one important observation can be made. Social workers' practice ideologies seem to bear very little resemblance indeed to what one might deduce from the social work literature and the content of social work courses. This problem is not confined to holders of unorthodox ideologies such as radical social work, or those working in untypical settings; it emerges clearly from the DHSS study (1978) of local authority and hospital social work. Halmos (1978a, p. 160) of course argued that inconsistency is actually built in to the ideologies of the counselling professions: '. . . The hallmark of the counsellor's faith is his refrainlike acceptance of contradictory positions, and incompatible canons of technique.'

It is, perhaps, a matter of opinion whether the distance between the general theoretical and practice ideologies in social work ultimately matters. One might say that practice ideologies are what we should really be concerned about; the rest is speculation. But we would take the view that it must eventually be extremely damaging to the credibility and effectiveness of social work if the bases of its social values and its assumptions about knowledge have drifted so far from what happens in the arena of practice. That is partly why we have advanced the idea of praxis as a bridge between theory and action. It is also our hope that entering into the topics of this book will reduce that gap.

Notes

Chapter 1   The person and moral agency

1   A work of this nature calls for fairly frequent use of third-person pronouns to indicate the position of persons in the abstract. The masculine forms are used here throughout to denote either sex. This usage may be unfashionable but it has the merits of neatness and simplicity, avoiding the uncomfortably ungrammatical ('they'), the tediously pedantic ('he/she') and the confusingly arbitrary ('he' or 'she' at random).

2   For a fuller discussion of determinism and morality, see Mackie (1977).

3   Glover (1977) gives an interesting discussion of this and related questions.

4   See Gowler (1972).

5   For discussions of the problem of relativism in social theory, see Benton (1977), Giddens (1976), Keat and Urry (1975).

6   See, for example, Jordan (1976, pp. 167–70); Statham (1978, chapter 2).

Chapter 2   Rights, self-determination, paternalism and authority

1   Obviously this is a simplification, the full conditions being somewhat complicated. For example, the child must be of a certain age and be dependent upon the parent; there are residence requirements; etc.

2   See Benn and Peters (1959, pp. 88–90) for a presentation of this argument.

3   Our discussion of paternalism was influenced by Bernard Williams's 1979 Seth Lecture at the University of Edinburgh.

4   See Day (1981) for an exploration of social control in the social work context.

5   For a fuller treatment of this subject, see Watt (1982).

Chapter 3   Moral and political theory in social work

1   A good many of the books listed in the bibliography are drawn from

121

these extensive fields. Useful introductions to moral philosophy are those of Frankena (1963), Raphael (1981), and Singer (1979). In political philosophy Gamble (1981), Goodwin (1982), and Raphael (1976) may serve as introductions. Weale (1983) is relevant for its direct application of political theory to the social welfare context.

2 Emmet (1979) gives an interesting discussion of varieties of moral theory and their relationship to each other, and presents an approach to resolving the antithesis set up here.

3 For the distinction we are using between a concept of justice and a conception of justice, see Rawls (1972, chapter I.1).

4 Political libertarianism, which advocates freedom from repression by human agency, should not be confused with philosophical libertarianism, which is a rejection of determinism.

5 See, for example, Porter (1980).

6 This conception of democracy as an *instrumental* value is not, however, universally held. Gamble (1981, p. 87) argues that the Jacobins 'took democracy as [the] starting point, the realisation of liberal values was secondary'. On this view the democratic participation of all citizens was of primary importance.

7 See, for example: Adler and Asquith (1981), Bolger et al. (1981), Corrigan and Leonard (1978), George and Wilding (1976), Jordan (1976), Plant, Lesser and Taylor-Gooby (1980), Taylor-Gooby and Dale (1981), Timms (1980), Wilding (1982).

8 See also Hampshire (1978b).

9 See Plant, Lesser and Taylor-Gooby (1980, chapters 1 and 9).

Chapter 4   Professional ethics and politics

1 See Downie and Telfer (1980, p. 162) for further discussion of 'ethics'.
2 The framework of this section follows Raphael (1976, chapter IV).
3 See, for example, DHSS (1978).
4 See Bernstein (1979) for an introduction to this subject.

Chapter 5   Ideology in social work

1 For an historical analysis of the term ideology, see Drucker (1974).
2 The following works on the philosophy of social science are relevant to an understanding of knowledge in social work: Benton (1977), Bernstein (1979), Hughes (1980), Keat and Urry (1975).

Bibliography

This bibliography lists all works referred to in the text and notes. It also includes a number of other works consulted in the preparation of this book and likely to be of interest to the student who wishes to read further in the subject areas covered.

Acton, H.B. (1970), *Kant's Moral Philosophy*, London, Macmillan.

Adler, M. and Asquith, S. (1981), *Discretion and Welfare*, London, Heinemann.

Ayer, A.J. (1963), *The Concept of a Person*, London, Macmillan.

Bailey, R. (1980), 'Social workers: pawns, police or agitators?' in Bailey and Brake (1980).

Bailey, R. and Brake, M. (1975), eds, *Radical Social Work*, London, Arnold.

Bailey, R. and Brake, M. (1980), eds, *Radical Social Work and Practice*, London, Arnold.

Barclay Committee (1982) see National Institute for Social Work (1982).

BASW (British Association for Social Workers) (n.d. – 1972?), *Social Action and Social Work*, Birmingham, BASW.

BASW (British Association of Social Workers) (1977), *The Social Work Task*, Birmingham, BASW.

Benn, S.I. and Peters, R.S. (1959), *Social Principles and the Democratic State*, London, Allen & Unwin.

Benton, T. (1977), *Philosophical Foundations of the Three Sociologies*, London, Routledge & Kegan Paul.

Berger, P.L. and Luckmann, T. (1971), *The Social Construction of Reality*, Harmondsworth, Penguin.

Berlin, I. (1969), 'Two concepts of liberty' in *Four Essays on Liberty*, Oxford University Press, reprinted in McDermott (1975).

Bernstein, R.J. (1971), *Praxis and Action*, Philadelphia, University of Pennsylvania.

Bernstein, R.J. (1979), *The Restructuring of Social and Political Theory*, London, Methuen.

Biestek, F.P. (1961), *The Casework Relationship*, London, Allen & Unwin.

Bibliography

Bolger, S., Corrigan, P., et al. (1981), *Towards Socialist Welfare Work*, London, Macmillan.

Broadie, A. (1978), 'Authority and the social caseworker', in Timms and Watson (1978).

Butrym, Z.T. (1976), *The Nature of Social Work*, London, Macmillan.

Campbell, A.V. (1975), *Moral Dilemmas in Medicine*, 2nd edition, Edinburgh, Churchill Livingstone.

Campbell, A.V. (1981), *Rediscovering Pastoral Care*, London, Darton, Longman & Todd.

Campbell, T.D. (1978), ' "Discretionary rights" ', in Timms and Watson (1978).

CCETSW (Central Council for Education and Training in Social Work) (1976), *Values in Social Work*, London, CCETSW.

Charvet, J. (1981), *A Critique of Freedom and Equality*, Cambridge University Press.

Chisholm, R.H. (1976), 'Human freedom and the self', in J. Bicke, ed., *Freedom and Morality*, University of Kansas.

Cockburn, C. (1978), *The Local State: Management of Cities and People*, London, Pluto.

Commission for International Development (1969), *Partners in Development*, Chairman L.B. Pearson, London, Pall Mall.

Corrigan, P., and Leonard, P. (1978), *Social Work Practice under Capitalism*, London, Macmillan.

Cranston, M. (1967), 'Human rights, real and supposed', in Raphael (1967), reprinted in Timms and Watson (1976).

Curnock, K. and Hardiker, P. (1979), *Towards Practice Theory: Skills and Methods in Social Assessment*, London, Routledge & Kegan Paul.

Davies, M. (1981), *The Essential Social Worker: A Guide to Positive Practice*, London, Heinemann.

Day, P.R. (1981), *Social Work and Social Control*, London, Tavistock.

DHSS (Department of Health and Social Security), UK (1978), *Social Service Teams: The Practitioners' View*, London, HMSO.

Downie, R.S. and Telfer, E. (1969), *Respect for Persons*, London, Allen & Unwin.

Downie, R.S. and Telfer, E. (1980), *Caring and Curing*, London, Methuen.

Drucker, H.M. (1974), *The Political Uses of Ideology*, London, Macmillan.

Dworkin, R. (1978), 'Liberalism', in Hampshire (1978a).

Emmet, D. (1967), 'Ethics and the social worker', in Younghusband (1967).

Emmet, D. (1979), *The Moral Prism*, London, Macmillan.

Feinberg, J. (1969), ed., *Moral Concepts*, Oxford University Press.

Feinberg, J. (1973a), *Social Philosophy*, Englewood Cliffs, N.J., Prentice-Hall.

Feinberg, J. (1973b), ed., *The Problem of Abortion*, Belmont, California, Wadsworth.

Frankena, W.K. (1963), *Ethics*, Englewood Cliffs, N.J., Prentice-Hall.

Freire, P. (1972), *Pedagogy of the Oppressed*, Harmondsworth, Penguin.

Freire, P. (1974), *Education as the Practice of Freedom*, London, Writers and Readers Publishing Cooperative.

Gamble, A. (1981), *An Introduction to Modern Social and Political Thought*, London, Macmillan.

Giddens, A. (1976), *New Rules of Sociological Method*, London, Hutchinson.

George, V. and Wilding, P. (1976), *Ideology and Social Welfare*, London, Routledge & Kegan Paul.

Giller, H. and Morris, A. (1981), ' "What type of case is this?" Social workers' decisions about children who offend' in Adler and Asquith (1981).

Glazer, N. (1968), 'The ideological uses of sociology', in Lazarsfeld, P.F., Sewell, W.H., and Wilensky, H.L. (1968), eds, *The Uses of Sociology*, London, Weidenfeld & Nicolson.

Glover, J. (1977), *Causing Death and Saving Lives*, Harmondsworth, Penguin.

Goodin, R.E. (1982), 'Freedom and the welfare state: theoretical foundations', *Journal of Social Policy*, vol. 11, no.2.

Goodwin, B. (1982), *Using Political Ideas*, Chichester, Wiley.

Gowler, D. (1972), 'On the concept of the person: a biosocial view', in Ruddock (1972).

Graham, K. (1982), ed., *Contemporary Political Philosophy: Radical Studies*, Cambridge University Press.

Gustafson, J.M. (1980), 'Mongolism, parental desires and the right to life' in Horan and Mall (1980).

Hadley, R. and Hatch, S. (1981), *Social Welfare and the Failure of the State*, London, Allen & Unwin.

Hadley, R. and McGrath, M. (1980), *Going Local: Neighbourhood Social Services*, London, Bedford Square Press.

Halmos, P. (1978a), *The Faith of the Counsellors*, 2nd edition, London, Constable.

Halmos, P. (1978b), *The Personal and the Political*, London, Hutchinson.

Hampshire, S. (1978a), ed., *Public and Private Morality*, Cambridge University Press.

Hampshire, S. (1978b), 'Morality and pessimism', in Hampshire (1978a).

Hardy, J.H. (1981), *Values in Social Policy: Nine Contradictions*, London, Routledge & Kegan Paul.

Horan D.J. and Mall, D. (1980), *Death, Dying and Euthanasia*, Frederick, Maryland, University Publications of America.

Hughes, J. (1980), *The Philosophy of Social Science*, London, Hutchinson.

Hunt, L. (1978), 'Social work and ideology', in Timms and Watson (1978).

Joad, C.E.M. (1938), *Guide to the Philosophy of Morals and Politics*, London, Gollancz.

Jones, H. (1975), ed., *Towards a New Social Work*, London, Routledge & Kegan Paul.

Jordan, B. (1976), *Freedom and the Welfare State*, London, Routledge & Kegan Paul.

Kant, I. (1962), Trans. T.K. Abbott, *Fundamental Principles of the Metaphysic of Ethics*, London, Longmans.

Keat, R. (1982), 'Liberal rights and socialism', in Graham (1982).

Keat, R. and Urry, J. (1975), *Social Theory as Science*, London, Routledge & Kegan Paul.

Bibliography

Laycock, J. (1981), 'Values and operating principles of the profession' in *Knowledge and Value Base of Social Work*, University of Toronto.
Leighton, N., Stalley, R., and Watson, D. (1982), *Rights and Responsibilities*, London, Heinemann.
Lewis, H. (1972), 'Morality and the politics of practice', *Social Casework*, vol. 53, no. 7, pp. 404–17.
MacCallum, G. (1967), 'Negative and positive freedom', *Philosophical Review*, vol. 76, no.3, pp. 312–45.
McDermott, F.E. (1975), ed., *Self-determination in Social Work*, London, Routledge & Kegan Paul.
Mackie, J.L. (1977), *Ethics: Inventing Right and Wrong*, Harmondsworth, Penguin.
Mannheim, K. (1960), *Ideology and Utopia*, London, Routledge & Kegan Paul.
Marris, P. (1974), *Loss and Change*, London, Routledge & Kegan Paul.
Midgley, J. (1981), *Professional Imperialism: Social Work in the Third World*, London, Heinemann.
Mill, J.S. (1962a), 'Utilitarianism', in Warnock (1962).
Mill, J.S. (1962b), 'On liberty', in Warnock (1962).
Mills, C.W. (1970), *The Sociological Imagination*, Harmondsworth, Penguin.
Morris, R. et al. (1971), eds, 'Profession of social work: code of ethics' in *Encyclopedia of Social Work*, 16th issue, New York, National Association of Social Workers.
National Institute for Social Work (1982), *Social Workers: Their Role and Tasks*, report of a working party: chairman P.M. Barclay. London, Bedford Square Press.
Nozick, R. (1974), *Anarchy, State and Utopia*, Oxford, Blackwell.
Parry, N., Rustin, M., and Satyamurti, C. (1979), eds, *Social Work, Welfare and the State*, London, Arnold.
Pearson, G. (1975a), *The Deviant Imagination*, London, Macmillan.
Pearson, G. (1975b), 'The politics of uncertainty: a study in the socialization of the social worker' in Jones (1975).
Pearson Report (1969), see Commission for International Development (1969).
Plamenatz, J. (1973), *Democracy and Illusion*, London, Longman.
Plant, R. (1970), *Social and Moral Theory in Casework*, London, Routledge & Kegan Paul.
Plant, R., Lesser, H., and Taylor-Gooby, P. (1980), *Political Philosophy and Social Welfare*, London, Routledge & Kegan Paul.
Porter, B.F. (1980), *The Good Life: Alternatives in Ethics*, New York, Macmillan.
Pritchard, C. and Taylor, R. (1978), *Social Work: Reform or Revolution?*, London, Routledge & Kegan Paul.
Quinton, A. (1967), ed., *Political Philosophy*, Oxford University Press.
Ragg, N. (1977), *People not Cases: A Philosophical Approach to Social Work*, London, Routledge & Kegan Paul.
Raphael, D.D. (1967), ed., *Political Theory and the Rights of Man*, London, Macmillan.

Raphael, D.D. (1976), *Problems of Political Philosophy*, revised edition, London, Macmillan.
Raphael, D.D. (1981), *Moral Philosophy*, Oxford University Press.
Rawls, J. (1972), *A Theory of Justice*, Oxford University Press.
Reamer, F.G. (1982), *Ethical Dilemmas in Social Service*, New York, Columbia University Press.
Rees, S. (1978), *Social Work Face to Face*, London, Arnold.
Ruddock, R. (1972), ed., *Six Approaches to the Person*, London, Routledge & Kegan Paul.
Ryan, A. (1981), 'John Rawls and his theory of justice', *New Society*, 5.2.81.
Ryle, G. (1973), *The Concept of Mind*, Harmondsworth, Penguin.
Satyamurti, C. (1981), *Occupational Survival*, Oxford, Blackwell.
SED/SHHD (Scottish Education Department, Scottish Home and Health Department), UK (1966), *Social Work and the Community*, Cmnd 3065, Edinburgh, HMSO.
Seebohm Report (1968), *Report of the Committee on Local Authority and Allied Social Services*, Cmnd 3703, London, HMSO.
Simpkin, M. (1979), *Trapped within Welfare*, London, Macmillan (2nd edition 1983).
Singer, P. (1979), *Practical Ethics*, Cambridge University Press.
Siporin, M. (1975), *Introduction to Social Work Practice*, New York, Macmillan.
Skinner, B.F. (1972), *Beyond Freedom and Dignity*, London, Cape.
Smith, G. (1980), *Social Need: Policy, Practice and Research*, London, Routledge & Kegan Paul.
Statham, D. (1978), *Radicals in Social Work*, London, Routledge & Kegan Paul.
Strauss, A. et al. (1964), *Psychiatric Ideologies and Institutions*, New York, Free Press.
Taylor-Gooby, P. and Dale, J. (1981), *Social Theory and Social Welfare*, London, Arnold.
Timms, N. (1980), ed., *Social Welfare: Why and How?*, London, Routledge & Kegan Paul.
Timms, N. (1983), *Social Work Values: An Enquiry*, London, Routledge & Kegan Paul.
Timms, N. and Timms, R. (1977), *Perspectives in Social Work*, London, Routledge & Kegan Paul.
Timms, N. and Watson, D. (1976), eds, *Talking about Welfare*, London, Routledge & Kegan Paul.
Timms, N. and Watson, D. (1978), eds, *Philosophy in Social Work*, London, Routledge & Kegan Paul.
Towle, C. (1945), *Common Human Needs*, ed. E. Younghusband (1973), London, Allen & Unwin.
United Nations (1948), *Universal Declaration of Human Rights*, UN.
Vlastos, G. (1969), 'Human worth, merit, and equality' in Feinberg (1969).
Warnock, M. (1962), ed., *Utilitarianism*, London, Collins.
Warnock, M. (1978), *Ethics since 1900*, 3rd edition, Oxford University Press.

Bibliography

Watson, D. (1980), *Caring for Strangers*, London, Routledge & Kegan Paul.

Watt, E.D. (1982), *Authority*, London, Croom Helm.

Weale, A. (1983), *Political Theory and Social Policy*, London, Macmillan.

Wilding, P. (1982), *Professional Power and Social Welfare*, London, Routledge & Kegan Paul.

Wilkes, R. (1981), *Social Work with Undervalued Groups*, London, Tavistock.

Younghusband, E. (1967), ed., *Social Work and Social Values*, London, Allen & Unwin.

Index

Numbers in italics refer to major sections.

abortion, 12, 13, 99
acceptance, 29, 32
accountability, 1, 6, 40, 41, 85, 89, 110;
  see also responsibility
action, 5, 8, 9, 10, 11, 14, 28, 30, 31, 33,
  34, 38, 42, 49, 50, 51, 57, 60, 68, 75,
  80, 86, 89, 90, 92, 94–8, 102–4, 120
Acton, H.B., 20
agape, 20
alienation, 101, 107
altruism, 64, 99
Aristotle, 95–6
authority, 5, 7, 23, 42–5, 66, 85, 106,
  111
Ayer, A.J., 14–15

Bailey, R., 35
Barclay Committee, 1, 62, 112, 114
BASW (British Association of Social
  Workers), 84–6, 89
behaviourism, 12, 54
Benn, S.I., 63
Bentham, J., 49
Berger, P., 102, 115
Berlin, I., 33, 60
Bernstein, R.J., 95–6
Beveridge, W., 107
Biestek, F.P., 2, 97–8
Bowlby, J., 17
Broadie, M., 43–4
Butrym, Z., 78, 84

Campbell, A.V., 6, 10, 11, 15, 20, 84, 85
Campbell, T.D., 27
capitalism, 71, 73, 74, 107, 109
CCETSW (Central Council for
  Education and Training in Social
  Work), 72
Charvet, J., 65
children, 9, 12–14, 16–18, 26, 30, 31,
  34, 35, 37–9, 44, 58, 121; child abuse,
  6, 28, 29, 31, 88, 100; children's
  homes, 12
Chisholm, R.H., 12, 77
Christianity, 20, 47, 63, 86, 112, 114
Cockburn, C., 88
collectivism, 73, 78, 107
communism, 69, 101, 107
community, 4, 17, 33, 41, 44, 52, 64, 67,
  71, 73, 76, 106, 110–13, 120
community social work, 62, 64, 111,
  112, 114
community work, 37, 64, 89, 111, 114,
  116, 119
compatibilism, 10, 60
confidentiality, 29, 32, 41, 93
consent, 91
consequentialism, 48–51, 53, 75, 79
conservatism, 69, 70, 87, 90, 102, 107
contract (political theory), see social
  contract
contract (in social work), see working
  agreement

Index

convention, 47–8
cooperation, 73
COS (Charity Organisation Society), 110
Cranston, M., 27
critical theory, 96
Curnock, K., 94

Davies, M., 76
Descartes, 14, 15; Cartesianism, 12
democracy, 65–6, 71, 122; democracies, 75, 88
deontology, 5, 48, 51–3, 59, 75, 77, 80; act and rule, 51
desert, 57
determinism, 9–13, 16, 33, 42, 60, 72, 119, 121, 122
deviance, 67, 77, 78, 109, 114
DHSS (Department of Health and Social Security), 38, 83, 89, 111, 120
Downie, R.S., 14, 20, 72, 77
dualism, 12, 14, 15
duties, 4, 20–2, 26, 28–9, 30, 37, 40, 41, 52, 54, 57, 85, 86, 93; of client, 34–5
Dworkin, R., 70

egalitarianism, 73, 80
Emmett, D., 86
equality, 55–60, 64–6, 73, 113
Erikson, E.H., 17
ethical egoism, 50
ethical theory, ethics, see moral theory
ethics, professional, 4, 21, 29–32, 82–7, 89, 98; codes of, 5, 83–6, 94
existentialism, 16, 51, 52
expediency, 67, 90, 98

Fabianism, 101
faith, 102, 106, 120
family, 10, 17, 35, 76, 106, 109, 110, 120
fascism, 57, 69
Feinberg, J., 12
fellowship, 55, 64–5, 113
feminism, 62
foetus, 12, 13, 18, 19
Frankena, W.K., 48, 52, 80
fraternity, 64, 73
freedom, 1, 4, 5, 8–10, 13, 15, 16, 23,
25, 27, 28, 33, 39, 49, 60–4, 65, 66, 71, 72, 78, 80, 90–2, 104, 113; negative, 33, 60–1, 62, 63, 70–4, 80, 108; positive, 33, 61–2, 63–5, 72, 73, 79, 80, 108
free will, 9, 10, 54, 60
Freire, P., 96–7
Freud, S., 17
Fromm, E., 72
functionalism, 78

Galbraith, J.K., 107
general will, 63, 91
Glazer, N., 101
good, 48–51, 55, 58, 61, 62, 66, 71, 73, 76, 77, 116; common, 59, 79, 92
Goodin, R.E., 63
Goodwin, B., 63, 66, 71, 72
Gustafson, J.M., 18

Habermas, J., 96
Hadley, R., 112
Halmos, P., 22, 97, 114, 120
happiness, 49, 50, 52, 65, 71, 76, 80
Hardiker, P., 96
harm, 92
Hatch, S., 112
Hayek, F.A., 71
Hegel, G.W.F., 63, 65
Hobbes, T., 54
humanism, 20, 118, 119
human nature, 8, 33
Hume, D., 115
Hunt, L., 102

ideology, 4, 5, 9, 30, 35, 70, 88, 97, 101–20, 122; practice, 103, 104, 119–20; practice oriented, 103, 104; professional, 103; scientific, 116, 117; theoretical, 104, 106, 115
imperatives, hypothetical and categorical, 52
individual(s), 2, 7–12, 14–17, 26, 29, 32, 47, 49, 50, 52, 53, 60–3, 65, 71, 73, 76, 78, 83, 88, 89, 101, 105, 107, 109, 110, 112–14, 120
individualisation, 29, 32, 86, 117
individualism, 10, 71, 72, 78, 106, 110–15

interests, 31, 32, 36–40, 49, 50, 52, 91, 92
intuitionism, 60

Joad, C.E.M., 112
justice, 5, 46, 50, 55–60, 64, 66, 79–81, 82, 92, 99, 109; distributive, 34, 58, 59, 62; as fairness, 57, 71, 73, 92; legal, 56, 92; retributive, 57; as right, 57, 71, 92; social, 4, 38, 56, 57, 71, 74, 92

Kant, I., 10, 20, 51, 52; Kantianism, 13, 20, 52, 53, 63, 72
Keat, R., 72
Keynes, J.M., 107
knowledge, 5, 6–8, 43, 44, 48, 84, 86, 93–100, 102, 104, 115–19, 120, 122

labour, 96; movement, 70, 82
Laing, R.D., 10
laissez-faire, 107
law, 9, 12, 25, 26, 27, 31, 32, 53, 66–8, 90–3, 113
Laycock, J., 7
learning theory, 12
Lewis, H., 8
liberalism, 5, 30, 38, 61–3, 69, 70–2, 73, 74, 77, 78, 80, 90, 92, 93, 102, 105, 114
liberation, 62
libertarianism, 9, 10, 33, 59, 60, 62, 70, 104, 119, 122
liberty, see freedom
Lothian Region, 82, 85, 86, 88, 89, 98, 115
love, 20–2, 47, 55
Luckmann, T., 102, 115

MacCallum, G., 63
McGrath, M., 112
Marcuse, H., 72, 96
Marris, P., 107
Marxism, 14, 69, 70, 72, 74, 75, 78, 90, 95, 96, 101, 105
mental handicap, 9, 14, 30, 33, 34
mental illness, 9, 14, 16, 30
mentally incompetent, 9, 30–2, 37, 58
merit, 59

meta-ethics, 117
Midgley, J., 18
Mill, J.S., 49, 62, 70, 71
Mills, C.W., 113
monism, 15
moral agency, 8–10, 13, 14, 19, 29, 31, 52, 54, 63, 64, 66, 117
morality, 2, 4, 7, 8, 14, 32, 35, 46, 50, 52, 54, 59, 65, 68, 71, 72, 75, 77, 80, 88, 92, 104, 115, 121; positive and critical, 47
moral theory, 3, 5, 19, 29, 40, 41, 46, 47–53, 79, 80, 83, 93, 95, 112, 113, 117, 118, 122
Morris, A., 103
Morris, R., 85

NASW (National Association of Social Workers), 84, 85, 94
Nozick, R., 71, 72, 107

obligation, 45, 48, 50, 52, 67, 68, 74, 75, 79, 83, 85, 90–3, 101, 110–12
offenders, 36, 37, 39, 49, 57–9, 110
operational philosophies, 103

person(s), 3, 4, 6, 7, 8–22, 23, 29, 33, 34, 36, 37, 41–3, 46, 47, 49, 52–4, 57, 58, 62, 64, 66, 71, 83, 95; becoming a, 16–18, 19; as biological entities, 12–13; as ends, 11, 19, 20, 24, 29, 30, 77; moral status of, 18–22, 47, 50; as rational beings, 13–14, 16, 19, 72, 118; respect for, 4, 7–11, 14, 19, 20, 21, 24, 29, 30, 31, 46, 47, 53, 71, 72, 77, 80, 83, 85–8, 97, 98, 114, 115, 117, 119; as self-conscious beings, 13, 14–16, 19, 118; as sentient beings, 13, 17
personal identity, 15–17
personality, 17
personhood, 4, 10–13, 16–20, 117
Peters, R.S., 63
pity, 20
Plamenatz, J., 65
Plant, R., 20, 77
political theory, 3, 5, 38, 40, 41, 46, 53–5, 66–75, 77–80, 88, 90, 95, 102, 112, 113, 117, 118

Index

politics, 2, *87–90*, 93, 104
polygamy, 68
positivism, 94, 95, 118, 119
poverty, 73, 77, 79, 84, 108, 111, 114, 115
power, 27, 35, 44, 48, 53, 66, 78, 85, 89, 90, 106, 109, 111, 115
practice principles, 7, 8, 38
practice theory, 94, 98, 116
praxis, 5, *95–100*, 104, 106, 109, 113, 115, 117, 120
problem solving, 97
professional distancing, 21
professional ideology, see ideology
professionalism, 6, 8, 78, 84, 106
professional judgement, 6, 27
professional relationship, 20–2
professional role, 29, 42, 78, 86, 93, 98, 106, 114, 115
prudence, 67, 68
psychoanalysis, 94, 111
punishment, 49, 57

Quinton, A., 66

radicalism, 63, 70, 79
radical social work, 96, *105–7*, 111, 120
Ragg, N., 6, 117
Raphael, D.D., 28, 87
Rawls, J., 56, 60, 80
Rees, S., 103, 119, 120
relativism, 18, 32, 102, 121
responsibility, 8, 23, 35, *40–5*, 78, 88, 91, 111, 115
Richmond, M., 95
rights (in general), 4, 5, 9, 20, *23–45*, 46, 54, 57, 61, 62, 72, 78, 85, 86, 101, 110
rights (specific): of civil disobedience, 27; to a competent service, 29, 33, 36; to free speech, 25, 26, 57, 58, 60; of intervention, 23, 35–8; to life, 12, 27, 28; of non-intervention, 38; of self-determination, 23, 28, 29, 31, 32, 39, 40
rights (types of): absolute, 24, 30, 33; of action, 28, 29, 37, 38; claim, 28; clients', *29–35*, 83, 85, 86; discretionary, 27; human, 23–7, 34, 58; legal, 23–8, 38, 44; moral, 23, 25,

26, 28, 38, 44, 80, 90; natural, 23, 24; nominal, 25–7; parents', 31; particular, 24, 25, 27, 28, 30–4; positive, 25–7; qualified, 24–8, 30–2, 34, 83; of recipience, 28, 29, 36–8; resource, 33, 34; universal, 24, 26–8, 30; welfare, 23, 25, 29, 33, 34, 37
Roe v. *Wade*, 12
Rogers, C., 101
Rousseau, J.-J., 63, 65
Ryan, A., 60
Ryle, G., 15

Satyamurti, C., 111
scientism, 7, 11, 21
SED/SHHD (Scottish Education Department/Scottish Home and Health Department), 111
Seebohm Report, 75, 76, 111, 114
self, 12, 17, 54, 113, 116
self-determination, 3, 4, 23, 29, 30–3, 38–40, 42, 87, 96, 98, 104, 108
Simpkin, M., 20
Singer, P., 13
Siporin, M., 86, 93
Skinner, B.F., 11, 12, 54
Smith, A., 107
Smith, G., 103, 120
social action, 89
social change, *107–9*
social control, 32, 36, 38–40, 78, 106, 115, 121
social democracy, 73
social engineering, 76, 116
socialisation, 16, 17
socialism, 5, 58, 63, 69, 72, *73–5*, 77–80, 102, 103, 105
social science, 7–9, 93–5, 97, 98, 112, 113, 116, 118
social welfare, 25, 57, 69, 88, 112
state, 26, 35, 39, 43, 53, 65–8, 71, 74, 78, 87–92, 101, 107, 111–13, 115, 117
Statham, D., 63, 72, 105
stranger, 47
Strathclyde Region, 83
Strauss, A., 103
strikes, 38, 99

technical principles, 7, 86, 94
techniques, 6, *115–19*
teleology, 47
Telfer, E., 14, 20, 72, 77
totalitarianism, 32
Towle, C., 55

United Nations, 25, 28
universality, 19, 52
utilitarianism, 5, 48–50, 59, 60, 71,
    75–81, 92; act and rule, 50
utility, 46, *79–81*, 99

values, 3–5, *6–8*, 23, 35, 45, 47, 54, 57,

63, 66, 77, 79, 81, 86, 91, 93–5, 96,
97, 102, 103, 105, 109, 114, 117, 119,
120; political, 54, *55–6*, 101, 102, 105
virtue, 59
Vlastos, G., 77
voluntary agencies, 88

Watson, D., 19
welfare benefits, 33, 89
welfare state, 27, 53, 55, 69, 75
Wilding, P., 107
Wilkes, R., 6, 10, 76, 117
working agreements, 35

Routledge Social Science Series

Routledge & Kegan Paul
London, Boston, Melbourne and Henley

Contents

International Library of Sociology 2
General Sociology 2
Foreign Classics of Sociology 3
Social Structure 3
Sociology and Politics 4
Criminology 4
Social Psychology 5
Sociology of the Family 5
Social Services 5
Sociology of Education 6
Sociology of Culture 6
Sociology of Religion 7
Sociology of Art and Literature 7
Sociology of Knowledge 7
Urban Sociology 7
Rural Sociology 8
Sociology of Industry and
Distribution 8
Anthropology 8
Sociology and Philosophy 9
International Library of
Anthropology 9
International Library of Phenomen-
ology and Moral Sciences 10
International Library of Social
Policy 10
International Library of Welfare and
Philosophy 11
Library of Social Work 11
Primary Socialization, Language and
Education 13
Reports of the Institute of
Community Studies 13
Reports of the Institute for Social
Studies in Medical Care 14
Medicine, Illness and Society 14
Monographs in Social Theory 14
Routledge Social Science Journals 14
Social and Psychological Aspects of
Medical Practice 15

*Authors wishing to submit manuscripts for any series
in this catalogue should send them to the Social Science Editor,
Routledge & Kegan Paul plc*

● *Books so marked are available in paperback also.*
○ *Books so marked are available in paperback only.*
*All books are in metric Demy 8vo format (216 × 138mm approx.)
unless otherwise stated.*

2

International Library of Sociology
General Editor John Rex

GENERAL SOCIOLOGY

Alexander, J. Theoretical Logic in Sociology.
Volume 1: Positivism, Presuppositions and Current Controversies. *234 pp.*
Volume 2: The Antinomies of Classical Thought: *Marx and Durkheim.*
Volume 3: The Classical Attempt at Theoretical Synthesis: *Max Weber.*
Volume 4: The Modern Reconstruction of Classical Thought: *Talcott Parsons.*
Barnsley, J. H. The Social Reality of Ethics. *464 pp.*
Brown, Robert. Explanation in Social Science. *208 pp.*
● Rules and Laws in Sociology. *192 pp.*
Bruford, W. H. Chekhov and His Russia. *A Sociological Study. 244 pp.*
Burton, F. and **Carlen, P.** Official Discourse. *On Discourse Analysis, Government Publications, Ideology. 160 pp.*
Cain, Maureen E. Society and the Policeman's Role. *326 pp.*
● **Fletcher, Colin.** Beneath the Surface. *An Account of Three Styles of Sociological Research. 221 pp.*
Gibson, Quentin. The Logic of Social Enquiry. *240 pp.*
Glassner, B. Essential Interactionism. *208 pp.*
Glucksmann, M. Structuralist Analysis in Contemporary Social Thought. *212 pp.*
Gurvitch, Georges. Sociology of Law. *Foreword by Roscoe Pound. 264 pp.*
Hinkle, R. Founding Theory of American Sociology 1881–1913. *376 pp.*
Homans, George C. Sentiments and Activities. *336 pp.*
Johnson, Harry M. Sociology: *A Systematic Introduction. Foreword by Robert K. Merton. 710 pp.*
● **Keat, Russell** and **Urry, John.** Social Theory as Science. *Second Edition. 278 pp.*
Mannheim, Karl. Essays on Sociology and Social Psychology. *Edited by Paul Kecskemeti. With Editorial Note by Adolph Lowe. 344 pp.*
Martindale, Don. The Nature and Types of Sociological Theory. *292 pp.*
● **Maus, Heinz.** A Short History of Sociology. *234 pp.*
Merquior, J. G. Rousseau and Weber. *A Study in the Theory of Legitimacy. 240 pp.*
Myrdal, Gunnar. Value in Social Theory: *A Collection of Essays on Methodology. Edited by Paul Streeten. 332 pp.*
Ogburn, William F. and **Nimkoff, Meyer F.** A Handbook of Sociology. *Preface by Karl Mannheim. 656 pp. 46 figures. 35 tables.*
Parsons, Talcott and **Smelser, Neil J.** Economy and Society: *A Study in the Integration of Economic and Social Theory. 362 pp.*
Payne, G., Dingwall, R., Payne, J. and **Carter, M.** Sociology and Social Research. *336 pp.*
Podgórecki, A. Practical Social Sciences. *144 pp.*
Podgórecki, A. and **Łos, M.** Multidimensional Sociology. *268 pp.*
Raffel, S. Matters of Fact. *A Sociological Inquiry. 152 pp.*
● **Rex, John.** Key Problems of Sociological Theory. *220 pp.*
Sociology and the Demystification of the Modern World. *282 pp.*
● **Rex, John.** (Ed.) Approaches to Sociology. *Contributions by Peter Abell, Frank Bechhofer, Basil Bernstein, Ronald Fletcher, David Frisby, Miriam Glucksmann, Peter Lassman, Herminio Martins, John Rex, Roland Robertson, John Westergaard and Jock Young. 302 pp.*
Rigby, A. Alternative Realities. *352 pp.*
Roche, M. Phenomenology, Language and the Social Sciences. *374 pp.*
Sahay, A. Sociological Analysis. *220 pp.*
Strasser, Hermann. The Normative Structure of Sociology. *Conservative and Emancipatory Themes in Social Thought. 286 pp.*

Strong, P. Ceremonial Order of the Clinic. *267 pp.*
Urry, J. Reference Groups and the Theory of Revolution. *244 pp.*
Weinberg, E. Development of Sociology in the Soviet Union. *173 pp.*

FOREIGN CLASSICS OF SOCIOLOGY

● **Gerth, H. H.** and **Mills, C. Wright.** From Max Weber: *Essays in Sociology. 502 pp.*
● **Tönnies, Ferdinand.** Community and Association (*Gemeinschaft und Gesellschaft*). *Translated and Supplemented by Charles P. Loomis. Foreword by Pitirim A. Sorokin. 334 pp.*

SOCIAL STRUCTURE

Andreski, Stanislav. Military Organization and Society. *Foreword by Professor A. R. Radcliffe-Brown. 226 pp. 1 folder.*
Bozzoli, B. The Political Nature of a Ruling Class. *Capital and Ideology in South Africa 1890–1939. 396 pp.*
Bauman, Z. Memories of Class. *The Prehistory and After life of Class. 240 pp.*
Broom, L., Lancaster Jones, F., McDonnell, P. and **Williams, T.** The Inheritance of Inequality. *208 pp.*
Carlton, Eric. Ideology and Social Order. *Foreword by Professor Philip Abrahams. 326 pp.*
Clegg, S. and **Dunkerley, D.** Organization, Class and Control. *614 pp.*
Coontz, Sydney H. Population Theories and the Economic Interpretation. *202 pp.*
Coser, Lewis. The Functions of Social Conflict. *204 pp.*
Crook, I. and **D.** The First Years of the Yangyi Commune. *304 pp., illustrated.*
Dickie-Clark, H. F. Marginal Situation: *A Sociological Study of a Coloured Group. 240 pp. 11 tables.*
Fidler, J. The British Business Elite. *Its Attitudes to Class, Status and Power. 332 pp.*
Giner, S. and **Archer, M. S.** (Eds) Contemporary Europe: *Social Structures and Cultural Patterns. 336 pp.*
● **Glaser, Barney** and **Strauss, Anselm L.** Status Passage: *A Formal Theory. 212 pp.*
Glass, D. V. (Ed.) Social Mobility in Britain. *Contributions by J. Berent, T. Bottomore, R. C. Chambers, J. Floud, D. V. Glass, J. R. Hall, H. T. Himmelweit, R. K. Kelsall, F. M. Martin, C. A. Moser, R. Mukherjee and W. Ziegel. 420 pp.*
Kelsall, R. K. Higher Civil Servants in Britain: *From 1870 to the Present Day. 268 pp. 31 tables.*
● **Lawton, Denis.** Social Class, Language and Education. *192 pp.*
McLeish, John. The Theory of Social Change. *Four Views Considered. 128 pp.*
● **Marsh, David C.** The Changing Social Structure of England and Wales, 1871–1961. *Revised edition. 288 pp.*
Menzies, Ken. Talcott Parsons and the Social Image of Man. *206 pp.*
● **Mouzelis, Nicos.** Organization and Bureaucracy. *An Analysis of Modern Theories. 240 pp.*
● **Ossowski, Stanislaw.** Class Structure in the Social Consciousness. *210 pp.*
● **Podgórecki, Adam.** Law and Society. *302 pp.*
Ratcliffe, P. Racism and Reaction. *A Profile of Handsworth. 388 pp.*
Renner, Karl. Institutions of Private Law and Their Social Functions. *Edited, with an Introduction and Notes, by O. Kahn-Freud. Translated by Agnes Schwarzschild. 316 pp.*
Rex, J. and **Tomlinson, S.** Colonial Immigrants in a British City. *A Class Analysis. 368 pp.*
Smooha, S. Israel. *Pluralism and Conflict. 472 pp.*
Strasser, H. and **Randall, S. C.** An Introduction to Theories of Social Change. *300 pp.*

Wesolowski, W. Class, Strata and Power. *Trans. and with Introduction by G. Kolankiewicz. 160 pp.*
Zureik, E. Palestinians in Israel. *A Study in Internal Colonialism. 264 pp.*

SOCIOLOGY AND POLITICS

Acton, T. A. Gypsy Politics and Social Change. *316 pp.*
Burton, F. Politics of Legitimacy. *Struggles in a Belfast Community. 250 pp.*
Crook, I. and **D.** Revolution in a Chinese Village. *Ten Mile Inn. 216 pp., illustrated.*
de Silva, S. B. D. The Political Economy of Underdevelopment. *640 pp.*
Etzioni-Halevy, E. Political Manipulation and Administrative Power. *A Comparative Study. 228 pp.*
Fielding, N. The National Front. *260 pp.*
● **Hechter, Michael.** Internal Colonialism. *The Celtic Fringe in British National Development, 1536–1966. 380 pp.*
Levy, N. The Foundations of the South African Cheap Labour System. *367 pp.*
Kornhauser, William. The Politics of Mass Society. *272 pp. 20 tables.*
● **Korpi, W.** The Working Class in Welfare Capitalism. *Work, Unions and Politics in Sweden. 472 pp.*
Kroes, R. Soldiers and Students. *A Study of Right- and Left-wing Students. 174 pp.*
Martin, Roderick. Sociology of Power. *214 pp.*
Merquior, J. G. Rousseau and Weber. *A Study in the Theory of Legitimacy. 286 pp.*
Myrdal, Gunnar. The Political Element in the Development of Economic Theory. *Translated from the German by Paul Streeten. 282 pp.*
Preston, P. W. Theories of Development. *296 pp.*
Varma, B. N. The Sociology and Politics of Development. *A Theoretical Study. 236 pp.*
Wong, S.-L. Sociology and Socialism in Contemporary China. *160 pp.*
Wootton, Graham. Workers, Unions and the State. *188 pp.*

CRIMINOLOGY

Ancel, Marc. Social Defence: *A Modern Approach to Criminal Problems. Foreword by Leon Radzinowicz. 240 pp.*
Athens, L. Violent Criminal Acts and Actors. *104 pp.*
Cain, Maureen E. Society and the Policeman's Role. *326 pp.*
Cloward, Richard A. and **Ohlin, Lloyd E.** Delinquency and Opportunity: *A Theory of Delinquent Gangs. 248 pp.*
Downes, David M. The Delinquent Solution. *A Study in Subcultural Theory. 296 pp.*
Friedlander, Kate. The Psycho-Analytical Approach to Juvenile Delinquency: *Theory, Case Studies, Treatment. 320 pp.*
Gleuck, Sheldon and **Eleanor.** Family Environment and Delinquency. *With the statistical assistance of Rose W. Kneznek. 340 pp.*
Lopez-Rey, Manuel. Crime. *An Analytical Appraisal. 288 pp.*
Mannheim, Hermann. Comparative Criminology: *A Text Book. Two volumes. 442 pp. and 380 pp.*
Morris, Terence. The Criminal Area: *A Study in Social Ecology. Foreword by Hermann Mannheim. 232 pp. 25 tables. 4 maps.*
Rock, Paul. Making People Pay. *338 pp.*
● **Taylor, Ian, Walton, Paul** and **Young, Jock.** The New Criminology. *For a Social Theory of Deviance. 325 pp.*
● **Taylor, Ian, Walton, Paul** and **Young, Jock.** (Eds) Critical Criminology. *268 pp.*

SOCIAL PSYCHOLOGY

Bagley, Christopher. The Social Psychology of the Epileptic Child. *320 pp.*
Brittan, Arthur. Meanings and Situations. *224 pp.*
Carroll, J. Break-Out from the Crystal Palace. *200 pp.*
● **Fleming, C. M.** Adolescence: Its Social Psychology. *With an Introduction to recent findings from the fields of Anthropology, Physiology, Medicine, Psychometrics and Sociometry. 288 pp.*
● The Social Psychology of Education: *An Introduction and Guide to Its Study. 136 pp.*
Linton, Ralph. The Cultural Background of Personality. *132 pp.*
● **Mayo, Elton.** The Social Problems of an Industrial Civilization. *With an Appendix on the Political Problem. 180 pp.*
Ottaway, A. K. C. Learning Through Group Experience. *176 pp.*
Plummer, Ken. Sexual Stigma. *An Interactionist Account. 254 pp.*
● **Rose, Arnold M.** (Ed.) Human Behaviour and Social Processes: *an Interactionist Approach. Contributions by Arnold M. Rose, Ralph H. Turner, Anselm Strauss, Everett C. Hughes, E. Franklin Frazier, Howard S. Becker et al. 696 pp.*
Smelser, Neil J. Theory of Collective Behaviour. *448 pp.*
Stephenson, Geoffrey M. The Development of Conscience. *128 pp.*
Young, Kimball. Handbook of Social Psychology. *658 pp. 16 figures. 10 tables.*

SOCIOLOGY OF THE FAMILY

Bell, Colin R. Middle Class Families: *Social and Geographical Mobility. 224 pp.*
Burton, Lindy. Vulnerable Children. *272 pp.*
Gavron, Hannah. The Captive Wife: *Conflicts of Household Mothers. 190 pp.*
George, Victor and **Wilding, Paul.** Motherless Families. *248 pp.*
Klein, Josephine. Samples from English Cultures.
  1. Three Preliminary Studies and Aspects of Adult Life in England. *447 pp.*
  2. Child-Rearing Practices and Index. *247 pp.*
Klein, Viola. The Feminine Character. *History of an Ideology. 244 pp.*
McWhinnie, Alexina M. Adopted Children. *How They Grow Up. 304 pp.*
● **Morgan, D. H. J.** Social Theory and the Family. *188 pp.*
● **Myrdal, Alva** and **Klein, Viola.** Women's Two Roles: *Home and Work. 238 pp. 27 tables.*
Parsons, Talcott and **Bales, Robert F.** Family: Socialization and Interaction Process. *In collaboration with James Olds, Morris Zelditch and Philip E. Slater. 456 pp. 50 figures and tables.*

SOCIAL SERVICES

Bastide, Roger. The Sociology of Mental Disorder. *Translated from the French by Jean McNeil. 260 pp.*
Carlebach, Julius. Caring for Children in Trouble. *266 pp.*
George, Victor. Foster Care. *Theory and Practice. 234 pp.*
  Social Security: *Beveridge and After. 258 pp.*
George, V. and **Wilding, P.** Motherless Families. *248 pp.*
● **Goetschius, George W.** Working with Community Groups. *256 pp.*
Goetschius, George W. and **Tash, Joan.** Working with Unattached Youth. *416 pp.*
Heywood, Jean S. Children in Care. *The Development of the Service for the Deprived Child. Third revised edition. 284 pp.*
King, Roy D., Ranes, Norma V. and **Tizard, Jack.** Patterns of Residential Care. *356 pp.*
Leigh, John. Young People and Leisure. *256 pp.*
● **Mays, John.** (Ed.) Penelope Hall's Social Services of England and Wales. *368 pp.*

Morris Mary. Voluntary Work and the Welfare State. *300 pp.*
Nokes. P. L. The Professional Task in Welfare Practice. *152 pp.*
Timms, Noel. Psychiatric Social Work in Great Britain (1939–1962). *280 pp.*
● Social Casework: *Principles and Practice. 256 pp.*

SOCIOLOGY OF EDUCATION

Banks, Olive. Parity and Prestige in English Secondary Education: a Study in
Educational Sociology. *272 pp.*
● Blyth, W. A. L. English Primary Education. *A Sociological Description.*
2. Background. *168 pp.*
Collier, K. G. The Social Purposes of Education: *Personal and Social Values in
Education. 268 pp.*
Evans, K. M. Sociometry and Education. *158 pp.*
● Ford, Julienne. Social Class and the Comprehensive School. *192 pp.*
Foster, P. J. Education and Social Change in Ghana. *336 pp. 3 maps.*
Fraser, W. R. Education and Society in Modern France. *150 pp.*
Grace, Gerald R. Role Conflict and the Teacher. *150 pp.*
Hans, Nicholas. New Trends in Education in the Eighteenth Century. *278 pp.
19 tables.*
● Comparative Education: *A Study of Educational Factors and Traditions. 360 pp.*
● Hargreaves, David. Interpersonal Relations and Education. *432 pp.*
● Social Relations in a Secondary School. *240 pp.*
School Organization and Pupil Involvement. *A Study of Secondary Schools.*
● Mannheim, Karl and Stewart, W. A. C. An Introduction to the Sociology of
Education. *206 pp.*
● Musgrove, F. Youth and the Social Order. *176 pp.*
● Ottaway, A. K. C. Education and Society: An Introduction to the Sociology of
Education. *With an Introduction by W. O. Lester Smith. 212 pp.*
Peers, Robert. Adult Education: *A Comparative Study. Revised edition. 398 pp.*
Stratta, Erica. The Education of Borstal Boys. *A Study of their Educational
Experiences prior to, and during, Borstal Training. 256 pp.*
● Taylor, P. H., Reid, W. A. and Holley, B. J. The English Sixth Form. *A Case
Study in Curriculum Research. 198 pp.*

SOCIOLOGY OF CULTURE

● Eppel, E. M. and M. Adolescents and Morality: *A Study of some Moral Values
and Dilemmas of Working Adolescents in the Context of a changing Climate
of Opinion. Foreword by W. J. H. Sprott. 268 pp. 39 tables.*
● Fromm, Erich. The Fear of Freedom. *286 pp.*
● The Sane Society. *400 pp.*
Johnson, L. The Cultural Critics. *From Matthew Arnold to Raymond Williams.
233 pp.*
Mannheim, Karl. Essays on the Sociology of Culture. *Edited by Ernst
Mannheim in co-operation with Paul Kecskemeti. Editorial Note by Adolph
Lowe. 280 pp.*
Structures of Thinking. *Edited by David Kettler, Volker Meja and Nico Stehr.
304 pp.*
Merquior, J. G. The Veil and the Mask. *Essays on Culture and Ideology.
Foreword by Ernest Gellner. 140 pp.*
Zijderfeld, A. C. On Clichés. *The Supersedure of Meaning by Function in
Modernity. 150 pp.*
Reality in a Looking Glass. *Rationality through an Analysis of Traditional
Folly. 208 pp.*

SOCIOLOGY OF RELIGION

Argyle, Michael and **Beit-Hallahmi, Benjamin.** The Social Psychology of Religion. *256 pp.*

Glasner, Peter E. The Sociology of Secularisation. *A Critique of a Concept. 146 pp.*

Hall, J. R. The Ways Out. *Utopian Communal Groups in an Age of Babylon. 280 pp.*

Ranson, S., Hinings, B. and **Bryman, A.** Clergy, Ministers and Priests. *216 pp.*

Stark, Werner. The Sociology of Religion. *A Study of Christendom.*
Volume II. *Sectarian Religion. 368 pp.*
Volume III. *The Universal Church. 464 pp.*
Volume IV. *Types of Religious Man. 352 pp.*
Volume V. *Types of Religious Culture. 464 pp.*

Turner, B. S. Weber and Islam. *216 pp.*

Watt, W. Montgomery. Islam and the Integration of Society. 230 pp.

Pomian-Srzednicki, M. Religious Change in Contemporary Poland. *Sociology and Secularization. 280 pp.*

SOCIOLOGY OF ART AND LITERATURE

Jarvie, Ian C. Towards a Sociology of the Cinema. *A Comparative Essay on the Structure and Functioning of a Major Entertainment Industry. 405 pp.*

Rust, Frances S. Dance in Society. *An Analysis of the Relationships between the Social Dance and Society in England from the Middle Ages to the Present Day. 256 pp. 8 pp. of plates.*

Schücking, L. L. The Sociology of Literary Taste. *112 pp.*

Wolff, Janet. Hermeneutic Philosophy and the Sociology of Art. *150 pp.*

SOCIOLOGY OF KNOWLEDGE

Diesing, P. Patterns of Discovery in the Social Sciences. *262 pp.*

● **Douglas, J. D.** (Ed.) Understanding Everyday Life. *270 pp.*

● **Hamilton, P.** Knowledge and Social Structure. *174 pp.*

Jarvie, I. C. Concepts and Society. *232 pp.*

Mannheim, Karl. Essays on the Sociology of Knowledge. *Edited by Paul Kecskemeti. Editorial Note by Adolph Lowe. 353 pp.*

Remmling, Gunter W. The Sociology of Karl Mannheim. *With a Bibliographical Guide to the Sociology of Knowledge, Ideological Analysis, and Social Planning. 255 pp.*

Remmling, Gunter W. (Ed.) Towards the Sociology of Knowledge. *Origin and Development of a Sociological Thought Style. 463 pp.*

Scheler, M. Problems of a Sociology of Knowledge. *Trans. by M. S. Frings. Edited and with an Introduction by K. Stikkers. 232 pp.*

URBAN SOCIOLOGY

Aldridge, M. The British New Towns. *A Programme Without a Policy. 232 pp.*

Ashworth, William. The Genesis of Modern British Town Planning: *A Study in Economic and Social History of the Nineteenth and Twentieth Centuries. 288 pp.*

Brittan, A. The Privatised World. *196 pp.*

Cullingworth, J. B. Housing Needs and Planning Policy: *a Restatement of the Problems of Housing Need and 'Overspill' in England and Wales. 232 pp. 44 tables. 8 maps.*

Dickinson, Robert E. City and Region: *A Geographical Interpretation. 608 pp. 125 figures.*
The West European City: *A Geographical Interpretation. 600 pp. 129 maps. 29 plates.*

Humphreys, Alexander J. New Dubliners: *Urbanization and the Irish Family. Foreword by George C. Homans. 304 pp.*

Jackson, Brian. Working Class Community: *Some General Notions raised by a Series of Studies in Northern England. 192 pp.*

● **Mann, P. H.** An Approach to Urban Sociology. *240 pp.*

Mellor, J. R. Urban Sociology in an Urbanized Society. *326 pp.*

Morris, R. N. and **Mogey, J.** The Sociology of Housing. *Studies at Berinsfield. 232 pp. 4 pp. plates.*

Mullan, R. Stevenage Ltd. *438 pp.*

Rex, J. and **Tomlinson, S.** Colonial Immigrants in a British City. *A Class Analysis. 368 pp.*

Rosser, C. and **Harris, C.** The Family and Social Change. *A Study of Family and Kinship in a South Wales Town. 352 pp. 8 maps.*

● **Stacey, Margaret, Batsone, Eric, Bell, Colin** and **Thurcott, Anne.** Power, Persistence and Change. *A Second Study of Banbury. 196 pp.*

RURAL SOCIOLOGY

● **Mayer, Adrian C.** Peasants in the Pacific. *A Study of Fiji Indian Rural Society. 248 pp. 20 plates.*

Williams, W. M. The Sociology of an English Village: *Gosforth. 272 pp. 12 figures. 13 tables.*

SOCIOLOGY OF INDUSTRY AND DISTRIBUTION

Dunkerley, David. The Foreman. *Aspects of Task and Structure. 192 pp.*

Eldridge, J. E. T. *Industrial Disputes. Essays in the Sociology of Industrial Relations. 288 pp.*

Hollowell, Peter G. The Lorry Driver. *272 pp.*

● **Oxaal, I., Barnett, T.** and **Booth, D.** (Eds) Beyond the Sociology of Development. *Economy and Society in Latin America and Africa. 295 pp.*

Smelser, Neil J. Social Change in the Industrial Revolution: *An Application of Theory to the Lancashire Cotton Industry, 1770–1840. 468 pp. 12 figures. 14 tables.*

Watson, T. J. The Personnel Managers. *A Study in the Sociology of Work and Employment, 262 pp.*

ANTHROPOLOGY

Brandel-Syrier, Mia. Reeftown Elite. *A Study of Social Mobility in a Modern African Community on the Reef. 376 pp.*

Dickie-Clark, H. F. The Marginal Situation. *A Sociological Study of a Coloured Group. 236 pp.*

Dube, S. C. Indian Village. *Foreword by Morris Edward Opler. 276 pp. 4 plates.*

India's Changing Villages: *Human Factors in Community Development. 260 pp. 8 plates. 1 map.*

Fei, H.-T. Peasant Life in China. *A Field Study of Country Life in the Yangtze Valley. With a foreword by Bronislaw Malinowski. 328 pp. 16 pp. plates.*

Firth, Raymond. Malay Fishermen. *Their Peasant Economy. 420 pp. 17 pp. plates.*

Gulliver, P. H. Social Control in an African Society: a Study of the Arusha, Agricultural Masai of Northern Tanganykia. *320 pp. 8 plates. 10 figures.* Family Herds. *288 pp.*

Jarvie, Ian C. The Revolution in Anthropology. *268 pp.*

Little, Kenneth L. Mende of Sierra Leone. *308 pp. and folder.*

Negroes in Britain. *With a New Introduction and Contemporary Study by Leonard Bloom. 320 pp.*

Tambs-Lyche, H. London Patidars. *168 pp.*
Madan, G. R. Western Sociologists on Indian Society. *Marx, Spencer, Weber, Durkheim, Pareto. 384 pp.*
Mayer, A. C. Peasants in the Pacific. *A Study of Fiji Indian Rural Society. 248 pp.*
Meer, Fatima. Race and Suicide in South Africa. *325 pp.*
Smith, Raymond T. The Negro Family in British Guiana: *Family Structure and Social Status in the Villages. With a Foreword by Meyer Fortes. 314 pp. 8 plates. 1 figure. 4 maps.*

SOCIOLOGY AND PHILOSOPHY

● Adriaansens, H. Talcott Parsons and the Conceptual Dilemma. *200 pp.*
Barnsley, John H. The Social Reality of Ethics. *A Comparative Analysis of Moral Codes. 448 pp.*
Diesing, Paul. Patterns of Discovery in the Social Sciences. *362 pp.*
● Douglas, Jack D. (Ed.) Understanding Everyday Life. *Toward the Reconstruction of Sociological Knowledge. Contributions by Alan F. Blum, Aaron W. Cicourel, Norman K. Denzin, Jack D. Douglas, John Heeren, Peter McHugh, Peter K. Manning, Melvin Power, Matthew Speier, Roy Turner, D. Lawrence Wieder, Thomas P. Wilson and Don H. Zimmerman. 370 pp.*
Gorman, Robert A. The Dual Vision. *Alfred Schutz and the Myth of Phenomenological Social Science. 240 pp.*
Jarvie, Ian C. Concepts and Society. *216 pp.*
Kilminster, R. Praxis and Method. *A Sociological Dialogue with Lukács, Gramsci and the Early Frankfurt School. 334 pp.*
Outhwaite, W. Concept Formation in Social Science. *255 pp.*
● Pelz, Werner. The Scope of Understanding in Sociology. *Towards a More Radical Reorientation in the Social Humanistic Sciences. 283 pp.*
Roche, Maurice, Phenomenology, Language and the Social Sciences. *371 pp.*
Sahay, Arun. Sociological Analysis. *212 pp.*
● Slater, P. Origin and Significance of the Frankfurt School. *A Marxist Perspective. 185 pp.*
Spurling, L. Phenomenology and the Social World. *The Philosophy of Merleau-Ponty and its Relation to the Social Sciences. 222 pp.*
Wilson, H. T. The American Ideology. *Science, Technology and Organization as Modes of Rationality. 368 pp.*

International Library of Anthropology
General Editor Adam Kuper

● Ahmed, A. S. Millennium and Charisma Among Pathans. *A Critical Essay in Social Anthropology. 192 pp.*
Pukhtun Economy and Society. *Traditional Structure and Economic Development. 422 pp.*
Barth, F. Selected Essays. *Volume 1. 256 pp.* Selected Essays. *Volume II. 200 pp.*
Brown, Paula. The Chimbu. *A Study of Change in the New Guinea Highlands. 151 pp.*
Duller, H. J. Development Technology. *192 pp.*
Foner, N. Jamaica Farewell. *200 pp.*
Gudeman, Stephen. Relationships, Residence and the Individual. *A Rural Panamanian Community. 288 pp. 11 plates, 5 figures, 2 maps, 10 tables.*
The Demise of a Rural Economy. *From Subsistence to Capitalism in a Latin American Village. 160 pp.*

Hamnett, Ian. Chieftainship and Legitimacy. *An Anthropological Study of Executive Law in Lesotho. 163 pp.*
Hanson, F. Allan. Meaning in Culture. *127 pp.*
Hazan, H. The Limbo People. *A Study of the Constitution of the Time Universe Among the Aged. 208 pp.*
Humphreys, S. C. Anthropology and the Greeks. *288 pp.*
Karp, I. Fields of Change Among the Iteso of Kenya. *140 pp.*
Kuper, A. Wives for Cattle. *Bridewealth in Southern Africa. 224 pp.*
Lloyd, P. C. Power and Independence. *Urban Africans' Perception of Social Inequality. 264 pp.*
Malinowski, B. and de la Fuente, J. Malinowski in Mexico. *The Economics of a Mexican Market System. Edited and Introduced by Susan Drucker-Brown. About 240 pp.*
Parry, J. P. Caste and Kinship in Kangra. *352 pp. Illustrated.*
Pettigrew, Joyce. Robber Noblemen. *A Study of the Political System of the Sikh Jats. 284 pp.*
Street, Brian V. The Savage in Literature. *Representations of 'Primitive' Society in English Fiction, 1858–1920. 207 pp.*
Van Den Berghe, Pierre L. Power and Privilege at an African University. *278 pp.*

International Library of Phenomenology and Moral Sciences
General Editor John O'Neill

Adorno, T. W. Aesthetic Theory. Translated by C. Lenhardt.
Apel, K.-O. Towards a Transformation of Philosophy. *308 pp.*
Bologh, R. W. Dialectical Phenomenology. *Marx's Method. 287 pp.*
Fekete, J. The Critical Twilight. *Explorations in the Ideology of Anglo-American Literary Theory from Eliot to McLuhan. 300 pp.*
Green, B. S. Knowing the Poor. *A Case Study in Textual Reality Construction. 200 pp.*
McHoul, A. W. How Texts Talk. *Essays on Reading and Ethnomethodology. 163 pp.*
Medina, A. Reflection, Time and the Novel. *Towards a Communicative Theory of Literature. 143 pp.*
O'Neill, J. Essaying Montaigne. *A Study of the Renaissance Institution of Writing and Reading. 244 pp.*
Schutz. A. Life Forms and Meaning Structure. *Translated, Introduced and Annotated by Helmut Wagner. 207 pp.*

International Library of Social Policy
General Editor Kathleen Jones

Bayley, M. Mental Handicap and Community Care. *426 pp.*
Bottoms, A. E. and McClean, J. D. Defendants in the Criminal Process. *284 pp.*
Bradshaw, J. The Family Fund. *An Initiative in Social Policy. 248 pp.*
Butler, J. R. Family Doctors and Public Policy. *208 pp.*
Davies, Martin. Prisoners of Society. *Attitudes and Aftercare. 204 pp.*
Gittus, Elizabeth. Flats, Families and the Under-Fives. *285 pp.*
Holman, Robert. Trading in Children. *A Study of Private Fostering. 355 pp.*
Jeffs, A. Young People and the Youth Service. *160 pp.*
Jones, Howard and Cornes, Paul. Open Prisons. *288 pp.*
Jones, Kathleen. History of the Mental Health Service. *428 pp.*

Jones, Kathleen with Brown, John, Cunningham, W. J., Roberts, Julian and Williams, Peter. Opening the Door. *A Study of New Policies for the Mentally Handicapped. 278 pp.*

Karn, Valerie. Retiring to the Seaside. *400 pp. 2 maps. Numerous tables.*

King, R. D. and Elliot, K. W. Albany: Birth of a Prison—End of an Era. *294 pp.*

Thomas, J. E. The English Prison Officer since 1850. *258 pp.*

Walton, R. G. Women in Social Work. *303 pp.*

● Woodward, J. To Do the Sick No Harm. *A Study of the British Voluntary Hospital System to 1875. 234 pp.*

International Library of Welfare and Philosophy
General Editors Noel Timms and David Watson

○ Campbell, J. The Left and Rights. *A Conceptual Analysis of the Idea of Socialist Rights. About 296 pp.*

● McDermott, F. E. (Ed.) Self-Determination in Social Work. *A Collection of Essays on Self-determination and Related Concepts by Philosophers and Social Work Theorists. Contributors: F. P. Biestek, S. Bernstein, A. Keith-Lucas, D. Sayer, H. H. Perelman, C. Whittington, R. F. Stalley, F. E. McDermott, I. Berlin, H. J. McCloskey, H. L. A. Hart, J. Wilson, A. I. Melden, S. I. Benn. 254 pp.*

● Plant, Raymond. Community and Ideology. *104 pp.*

● Plant, Raymond, Lesser, Harry and Taylor-Gooby, Peter. Political Philosophy and Social Welfare. *Essays on the Normative Basis of Welfare Provision. 276 pp.*

Ragg, N. M. People Not Cases. *A Philosophical Approach to Social Work. 168 pp.*

Timms, Noel (Ed.) Social Welfare. *Why and How? 316 pp. 7 figures.*

● Timms, Noel and Watson, David (Eds) Talking About Welfare. *Readings in Philosophy and Social Policy. Contributors: T. H. Marshall, R. B. Brandt, G. H. von Wright, K. Nielsen, M. Cranston, R. M. Titmuss, R. S. Downie, E. Telfer, D. Donnison, J. Benson, P. Leonard. A. Keith-Lucas, D. Walsh, I. T. Ramsey. 230 pp.*

● Philosophy in Social Work. *250 pp.*

● Weale, A. Equality and Social Policy. *164 pp.*

Library of Social Work
General Editor Noel Timms

● Baldock, Peter. Community Work and Social Work. *140 pp.*

○ Beedell, Christopher. Residential Life with Children. *210 pp. Crown 8vo.*

● Berry, Juliet. Daily Experience in Residential Life. *A Study of Children and their Care-givers. 202 pp.*

○ Social Work with Children. *190 pp. Crown 8vo.*

● Brearley, C. Paul. Residential Work with the Elderly. *116 pp.*

● Social Work, Ageing and Society. *126 pp.*

● Cheetham, Juliet. Social Work with Immigrants. *240 pp. Crown 8vo.*

● Cross, Crispin P. (Ed.) Interviewing and Communication in Social Work. *Contributions by C. P. Cross, D. Laurenson, B. Strutt, S. Raven. 192 pp. Crown 8vo.*

● Curnock, Kathleen and Hardiker, Pauline. Towards Practice Theory. *Skills and Methods in Social Assessments. 208 pp.*

● Davies, Bernard. The Use of Groups in Social Work Practice. *158 pp.*

Davies, Bleddyn and Knapp, M. Old People's Homes and the Production of Welfare. *264 pp.*

● **Davies, Martin.** Support Systems in Social Work. *144 pp.*
Ellis, June. (Ed.) West African Families in Britain. *A Meeting of Two
Cultures. Contributions by Pat Stapleton, Vivien Biggs. 150 pp. 1 map.*
○ **Ford, J.** Human Behaviour. *Towards a Practical Understanding. About
160 pp.*
● **Hart, John.** Social Work and Sexual Conduct. *230 pp.*
Heraud, Brian. Training for Uncertainty. *A Sociological Approach to Social
Work Education. 138 pp.*
Holder, D. and **Wardle, M.** Teamwork and the Development of a Unitary
Approach. *212 pp.*
● **Hutten, Joan M.** Short-Term Contracts in Social Work. *Contributions by Stella
M. Hall, Elsie Osborne, Mannie Sher, Eva Sternberg, Elizabeth Tuters.
134 pp.*
Jackson, Michael P. and **Valencia, B. Michael.** Financial Aid Through Social
Work. *140 pp.*
● **Jones, Howard.** The Residential Community. *A Setting for Social Work.
150 pp.*
● (Ed.) Towards a New Social Work. *Contributions by Howard Jones, D. A.
Fowler, J. R. Cypher, R. G. Walton, Geoffrey Mungham, Philip Priestley,
Ian Shaw, M. Bartley, R. Deacon, Irwin Epstein, Geoffrey Pearson.
184 pp.*
Jones, Ray and **Pritchard, Colin.** (Eds) Social Work With Adolescents.
*Contributions by Ray Jones, Colin Pritchard, Jack Dunham, Florence
Rossetti, Andrew Kerslake, John Burns, William Gregory, Graham
Templeman, Kenneth E. Reid, Audrey Taylor.*
○ **Jordon, William.** The Social Worker in Family Situations. *160 pp. Crown 8vo.*
● **Laycock, A. L.** Adolescents and Social Work. *128 pp. Crown 8vo.*
● **Lees, Ray.** Politics and Social Work. *128 pp. Crown 8vo.*
● Research Strategies for Social Welfare. *112 pp. Tables.*
○ **McCullough, M. K.** and **Ely, Peter J.** Social Work with Groups. *127 pp. Crown
8vo.*
● **Moffett, Jonathan.** Concepts in Casework Treatment. *128 pp. Crown 8vo.*
Parsloe, Phyllida. Juvenile Justice in Britain and the United States. *The
Balance of Needs and Rights. 336 pp.*
● **Plant, Raymond.** Social and Moral Theory in Casework. *112 pp. Crown 8vo.*
Priestley, Philip, Fears, Denise and **Fuller, Roger.** Justice for Juveniles. *The
1969 Children and Young Persons Act: A Case for Reform? 128 pp.*
● **Pritchard, Colin** and **Taylor, Richard.** Social Work: Reform or Revolution?
170 pp.
○ **Pugh, Elisabeth.** Social Work in Child Care. *128 pp. Crown 8vo.*
● **Robinson, Margaret.** Schools and Social Work. *282 pp.*
○ **Ruddock, Ralph.** Roles and Relationships. *128 pp. Crown 8vo.*
● **Sainsbury, Eric.** Social Diagnosis in Casework. *118 pp. Crown 8vo.*
● **Sainsbury, Eric, Phillips, David** and **Nixon, Stephen.** Social Work in Focus.
*Clients' and Social Workers' Perceptions in Long-Term Social Work.
220 pp.*
● Social Work with Families. *Perceptions of Social Casework among Clients of a
Family Service. 188pp.*
Seed, Philip. The Expansion of Social Work in Britain. *128 pp. Crown 8vo.*
● **Shaw, John.** The Self in Social Work. *124 pp.*
Smale, Gerald G. Prophecy, Behaviour and Change. *An Examination of Self-
fulfilling Prophecies in Helping Relationships. 116 pp. Crown 8vo.*
Smith, Gilbert. Social Need. *Policy, Practice and Research. 155 pp.*
● Social Work and the Sociology of Organisations. *124 pp. Revised edition.*
● **Sutton, Carole.** Psychology for Social Workers and Counsellors. *An
Introduction. 248 pp.*
● **Timms, Noel.** Language of Social Casework. *122 pp. Crown 8vo.*

● Recording in Social Work. *124 pp. Crown 8vo.*
● **Todd, F. Joan.** Social Work with the Mentally Subnormal. *96 pp. Crown 8vo.*
● **Walrond-Skinner, Sue.** Family Therapy. *The Treatment of Natural Systems.*
   172 pp.
● **Warham, Joyce.** An Introduction to Administration for Social Workers.
   Revised edition. 112 pp.
● An Open Case. *The Organisational Context of Social Work. 172 pp.*
○ **Wittenberg, Isca Salzberger.** Psycho-Analytic Insight and Relationships.
   A Kleinian Approach. 196 pp. Crown 8vo.

Primary Socialization, Language and Education

General Editor   Basil Bernstein

Adlam, Diana S., *with the assistance of Geoffrey Turner and Lesley Lineker.*
   Code in Context. *272 pp.*
Bernstein, Basil. Class, Codes and Control. *3 volumes.*
●   1. *Theoretical Studies Towards a Sociology of Language. 254 pp.*
    2. *Applied Studies Towards a Sociology of Language. 377 pp.*
●   3. *Towards a Theory of Educational Transmission. 167 pp.*
Brandis, Walter and **Henderson, Dorothy.** Social Class, Language and
   Communication. *288 pp.*
Cook-Gumperz, Jenny. Social Control and Socialization. *A Study of Class*
   Differences in the Language of Maternal Control. 290 pp.
● **Gahagan, D. M.** and **G. A.** Talk Reform. *Exploration in Language for Infant*
   School Children. 160 pp.
Hawkins, P. R. Social Class, the Nominal Group and Verbal Strategies. *About*
   220 pp.
Robinson, W. P. and **Rakstraw, Susan D. A.** A Question of Answers.
   2 volumes. 192 pp. and 180 pp.
Turner, Geoffrey J. and **Mohan, Bernard A.** A Linguistic Description and
   Computer Programme for Children's Speech. *208 pp.*

Reports of the Institute of Community Studies

Baker, J. The Neighbourhood Advice Centre. *A Community Project in*
   Camden. 320 pp.
● **Cartwright, Ann.** Patients and their Doctors. *A Study of General Practice.*
   304 pp.
Dench, Geoff. Maltese in London. *A Case-study in the Erosion of Ethnic*
   Consciousness. 302 pp.
Jackson, Brian and **Marsden, Dennis.** Education and the Working Class: *Some*
   General Themes Raised by a Study of 88 Working-class Children in a
   Northern Industrial City. 268 pp. 2 folders.
Madge, C. and **Willmott, P.** Inner City Poverty in Paris and London. *144 pp.*
Marris, Peter. The Experience of Higher Education. *232 pp. 27 tables.*
● Loss and Change. *192 pp.*
Marris, Peter and **Rein, Martin.** Dilemmas of Social Reform. *Poverty and*
   Community Action in the United States. 256 pp.
Marris, Peter and **Somerset, Anthony.** African Businessmen. *A Study of*
   Entrepreneurship and Development in Kenya. 256 pp.
Mills, Richard. Young Outsiders: *a Study in Alternative Communities. 216 pp.*
Runciman, W. G. Relative Deprivation and Social Justice. *A Study of Attitudes*
   to Social Inequality in Twentieth-Century England. 352 pp.

Willmott, Peter. Adolescent Boys in East London. *230 pp.*
Willmott, Peter and **Young, Michael.** Family and Class in a London Suburb. *202 pp. 47 tables.*
Young, Michael and **McGeeney, Patrick.** Learning Begins at Home. *A Study of a Junior School and its Parents. 128 pp.*
Young, Michael and **Willmott, Peter.** Family and Kinship in East London. *Foreword by Richard M. Titmuss. 252 pp. 39 tables.*
The Symmetrical Family. *410 pp.*

Reports of the Institute for Social Studies in Medical Care

Cartwright, Ann, Hockey, Lisbeth and **Anderson, John J.** Life Before Death. *310 pp.*
Dunnell, Karen and **Cartwright, Ann.** Medicine Takers, Prescribers and Hoarders. *190 pp.*
Farrell, C. My Mother Said. . . *A Study of the Way Young People Learned About Sex and Birth Control. 288 pp.*

Medicine, Illness and Society
General Editor W. M. Williams

Hall, David J. Social Relations & Innovation. *Changing the State of Play in Hospitals. 232 pp.*
Hall, David J. and **Stacey M.** (Eds) Beyond Separation. *234 pp.*
Robinson, David. The Process of Becoming Ill. *142 pp.*
Stacey, Margaret *et al.* Hospitals, Children and Their Families. *The Report of a Pilot Study. 202 pp.*
Stimson, G. V. and **Webb, B.** Going to See the Doctor. *The Consultation Process in General Practice. 155 pp.*

Monographs in Social Theory
General Editor Arthur Brittan

● **Barnes, B.** Scientific Knowledge and Sociological Theory. *192 pp.*
Bauman, Zygmunt. Culture as Praxis. *204 pp.*
● **Dixon, Keith.** Sociological Theory. *Pretence and Possibility. 142 pp.*
The Sociology of Belief. *Fallacy and Foundation. 144 pp.*
Goff, T. W. Marx and Mead. *Contributions to a Sociology of Knowledge. 176 pp.*
Meltzer, B. N., Petras, J. W. and **Reynolds, L. T.** Symbolic Interactionism. *Genesis, Varieties and Criticisms. 144 pp.*
● **Smith, Anthony D.** The Concept of Social Change. *A Critique of the Functionalist Theory of Social Change. 208 pp.*
● **Tudor, Andrew.** Beyond Empiricism. *Philosophy of Science in Sociology. 224 pp.*

Routledge Social Science Journals

The British Journal of Sociology. *Editor – Angus Stewart; Associate Editor – Leslie Sklair. Vol. 1, No. 1 – March 1950 and Quarterly. Roy. 8vo. All back issues available. An international journal publishing original papers in the field of sociology and related areas.*

Community Work. *Edited by David Jones and Majorie Mayo. 1973. Published annually.*
Economy and Society. *Vol. 1, No. 1. February 1972 and Quarterly. Metric Roy. 8vo. A journal for all social scientists covering sociology, philosophy, anthropology, economics and history. All back numbers available.*
Ethnic and Racial Studies. *Editor – John Stone. Vol. 1 – 1978. Published quarterly.*
Religion. Journal of Religion and Religions. *Chairman of Editorial Board, Ninian Smart. Vol. 1, No. 1, Spring 1971. A journal with an interdisciplinary approach to the study of the phenomena of religion. All back numbers available.*
Sociological Review. *Chairman of Editorial Board, S. J. Eggleston. New Series. August 1982, Vol. 30, No. 1. Published quarterly.*
Sociology of Health and Illness. *A Journal of Medical Sociology. Editor – Alan Davies; Associate Editor – Ray Jobling. Vol. 1, Spring 1979. Published 3 times per annum.*
Year Book of Social Policy in Britain. *Edited by Kathleen Jones. 1971. Published annually.*

Social and Psychological Aspects of Medical Practice
Editor Trevor Silverstone

Lader, Malcolm. Psychophysiology of Mental Illness. *280 pp.*
● **Silverstone, Trevor** and **Turner, Paul.** Drug Treatment in Psychiatry. *Third edition. 256 pp.*
Whiteley, J. S. and **Gordon, J.** Group Approaches in Psychiatry. *240 pp.*